ROBUST in love

MY BRAVE HEART JOURNEY

Brooke Robertson

This is an IndieMosh book

brought to you by MoshPit Publishing
an imprint of Mosher's Business Support Pty Ltd

PO Box 147
Hazelbrook NSW 2779

indiemosh.com.au

 A catalogue record for this work is available from the National Library of Australia

Title: Robust in Love

Subtitle   My Brave Heart Journey

Author: Robertson, Brooke (1995–)

ISBNs: 978-1-922368-48-5 (paperback)
            978-1-922368-49-2 (ebook – epub)
            978-1-922368-50-8 (ebook – mobi)

Subjects: RELIGION: Christian living – Personal memoirs; BIOGRAPHY & AUTOBIOGRAPHY: Personal memoirs; FAMILY & RELATIONSHIPS: General

Cover design and layout: Brooke Robertson and Ally Mosher @allymosher.com

Internal and back images: © Shivneel Kumar @shiveeykaay

Edited by Shana Leigh McKibben

*This book is dedicated to my two Goddaughters
Scotland 'Scottie' Rose & Michal 'Monkey' Reece;
I pray that the influence of my life will always inspire you girls
to pursue Jesus.
(And eat ice cream behind your parents' back!)*

CONTENTS

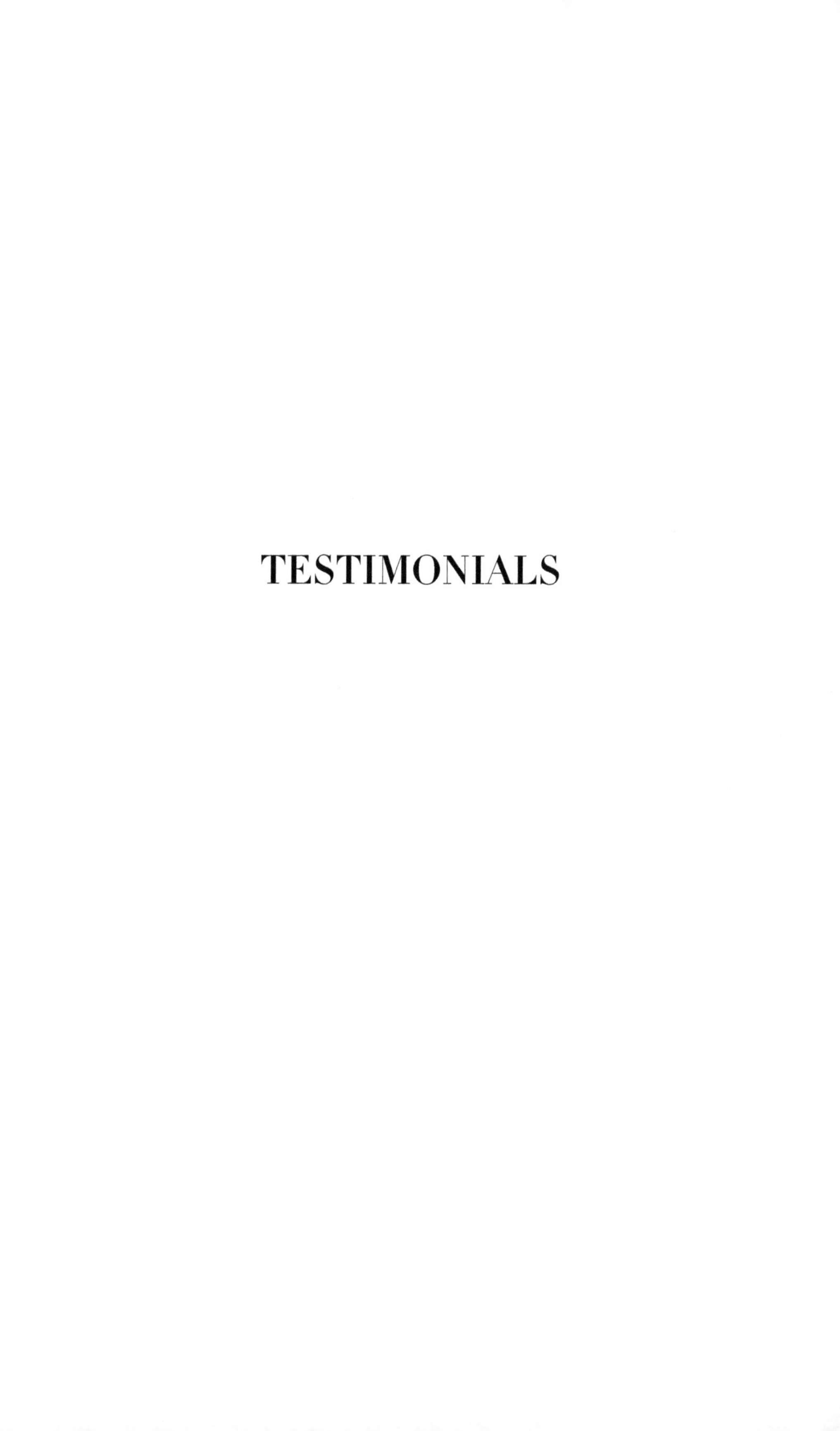

TESTIMONIALS

I feel honoured and privileged that I got to read the pages of this very personal diary. This book is one of the best books that I have read in a while. I was on the edge of my seat the whole way, my curiosity needing to be staved! What is bravery? What does it mean to be robust in love? How does someone go through really hard life experiences and come out of it in a better place – spiritually, emotionally and physically – than when they began?

I was so engaged, in fact, that I had to read it all in one sitting! Brooke keeps you captivated; sharing her vulnerable and raw experiences of a life filled with hardship, forgiveness, friends, bravery, renewing of the heart, and learning to be robust in love. And did I mention that somehow, amongst all this, she managed to crack me up with her hilarious sense of humour?! I truly felt like I was at coffee with my best friend.

There are moments in her stories where you want to cry and moments where you will laugh, but I can guarantee you that this thought-provoking book will have you questioning and checking your own mind, heart and spiritual state until the very last page. Boy, did I get convicted to check my heart! Incredibly relatable and yet entirely her own, this book is a must-read.

Brooke has so artfully and masterfully crafted her heart onto the pages of this book and I truly believe that it is the work of Holy Spirit that has allowed her to embrace her experiences not with bitterness, but with a true meaning of what it is to love and be loved. It brought me to my knees in worship before The King.

Reading this book was a crazy ride and I can't wait to do it all again!

This raw and honest true story of Brooke's consists of bravery, resilience and determination. Her story and faith will inspire you to see through every personal struggle or challenge you yourself may face, knowing a Greater Love is always beside you and walking with you till the end.

For starters you will find yourself, within a very short time of reading, falling in deep admiration for Brooke and wishing you had her in your corner. She is as real as they come as you will soon discover. This fiery powerhouse has a fierce, unwavering commitment to God, her family and those she loves. Everything about her is undeniably marked by her tenacity to walk in robust love. Her story will lift you up, cause you to laugh, cry, be inspired and help you in becoming a person of greater character and bravery. With every penned word, Brooke masterfully crafts her life's story in a tangible, heartfelt passion that beckons change in your own. I am honoured to know her, blessed to call her friend and humbled she would openly share her life's story to whoever needs a shoulder to rest on. God's hand has been on her before, during and after every season of life. Let her story lead you to the Father's heart and discover who God is and how He is using your challenge for triumph and purpose.

Emilio Bonilla. Boston, USA

You are holding pages that once you've read, you cannot unread. These precious pages straight from Brooke's heart exemplify vulnerability, raw honesty, and beckon us all onto the construction site of bravery and the operating table of healing. She has written with an honesty that is almost scary, but her voice is one of grace and love (let's not forget humour!) guiding us further into the Father's arms and onto a worn pathway towards wholeness.

Thank you for your bravery, Brooke. Thank you for writing this book.

Karen Brink. Ontario, Canada

B sat across from me a couple of years ago at a cafe, much like she will invite you to do as you begin reading, beckoning you to grab a coffee as you get comfortable. B sipped a soy mocha on our first coffee date, I won't hold that against her if you won't. I am an avid long black drinker but for some strange reason that day I replicated another's coffee order. One of the first drops I felt in my spirit from being around her was, 'B can be trusted' … despite what I now found myself sipping!

Reader, you will trace her life through this book and find her loyalty to Jesus and His leading tangible on every page. I remember in the early days of our friendship, in one of her first detailed messages, she explained why she included a purple heart emoticon in her consistent daily messages. She explained that purple hearts were a symbol of bravery, particularly in the sphere of soldiers at battle, signifying bravery from being wounded when fighting a battle. She declared a purple heart over me and I dwelt on the security knowing she herself had earned a purple heart, clearly of bravery and clearly of love. But as time has unravelled more, the title of this book parallels so profoundly with a resolve she has made and clings to daily.

When a friend is going through a painful time, most of us stand at the end of the tunnel and encourage them that there is light and there is hope and to follow our voice to recovery. Not B, she is willing to be found in the trenches next to you, digging away at refined gold beneath the surface. Time and time again she overturns soil, ridden in loyalty and sacrifice, sticking it out through the seasons.

My prayer is that this book reveals the B I have come to know; dear reader, she is a friend to be trusted. As your eyes pave the way through every sentence and chapter, let your heart trace His faithfulness throughout her life and her brave, robust love that is etched into every detail.

Thank you B, for staying and remaining faithful to all Jesus asks of you. For this we have this book and heaven knows the secret place you entered time and time again to come out the other side with not just robust love, but your story bound up to now display profound wells of revelation.

There's a private place reserved for the lovers of God, where they sit near Him and receive the revelation secrets of His promises.
Psalm 25:14 (TPT)

Claire Stanmore. Noosa, Australia

When you first encounter Brooke Robertson her physical beauty is disarming. You would even be forgiven for expecting a conceited and self-centred person, as often happens in such cases. But the moment she greets you, asks you your name and begins to engage with you in her larger-than-life way, you realise that what you see on the outside pales in significance to her inner beauty. This girl, so young in years but so solid and grounded, is the *real deal*. Her family is the real deal. She loves without reserve, even though life so far has given her so many reasons to withhold. She has chosen to rise above – to learn from her mistakes and to fight against all odds to get her hands on all that God has purposed for her.

Brave and full of tenacity, Brooke will have you laughing hysterically and then a moment later in floods of tears. Her story only speaks of a hope unswerving. It has been such an honour to work with this talented, vulnerable and authentic author. I believe there is so much more to come!

Thank you, dear Brooke, for putting your treasure in my hands and allowing me to edit for you. This is more than just your words; it is your heart written in ink on a page. I am so proud of you.

Shana McKibben. Newcastle, Australia

FOREWORD

I will never forget the moment Brooke told me she was in the middle of writing a book. I was shocked and so proud all at the same time. Shocked because I had yet to meet anyone so young who had written a book. Proud because she would be the first person I knew at such a young age to have written a book.

Before Brooke could tell me what the book was about, I tried to guess what she would possibly want to write about. Would she decide to follow in the footsteps of some of the world's most notable authors and write the next Harry Potter series? Or would it be the romance novel that you can't seem to put down? None of my guesses proved to be right and boy was I glad they were wrong.

Brooke had chosen to write about something greater. Something I knew would be powerful enough to touch the hearts of the people she knew and people she would never know. Brooke, to my pleasant surprise, had chosen to tell her story. Oh man, how did I not guess this first? Brooke was one of the most tenacious, persevering and unwavering young ladies I knew. Why wouldn't she share her story with the world? Her voice had always been one that spoke with love, conviction, and truth. And throughout the many years I have known Brooke, I have seen her live a life that spoke louder than her words. A life that loved and served others. A life that loved

God and sought to live for him daily. A life that would go through plenty of ups and downs but still remain standing in the end. It would be a life that would now have the opportunity to speak for itself through the pages of this book.

This book unfolds a powerful story of discovery, truth, and love. It is a journey through the personal diary of a young woman's battle to continue to keep standing. How does one not give up when life throws you curveballs and God does not seem to be answering any of your phone calls? These are some of life's most pressing questions that many can't seem to find the answers to. Nonetheless, it is through the pages of this book that readers get a glimpse into a series of God-given revelations and truths of God's power and grace that can sustain and empower anyone through life's toughest moments. *Robust in Love* is a raw and unfiltered account of life's toughest times. It is a story of faith, perseverance and strength despite all odds. It is one girl's journey that will leave you inspired and encouraged to never give up.

Niyah Rahmaan. Los Angeles, USA

* * *

Cultivating a book, like gardening, takes planning, planting and pruning. It requires nature, nurture and sweat. It means approaching blank pages with trepidation. It has been a bumpy, dusty and difficult road but it has not been without its fair share of sunlight, showers and the not-so-occasional dash of fertiliser. I am hugely grateful to Brooke for opening her garden gate and letting us into her private life – for giving us a snapshot of her heart and the reasons why it beats so strongly for her family, her friends and not least of all, her Saviour. She has delved so deeply within herself to bring these revelations to life; far deeper than has felt comfortable or safe.

Brooke has so generously dedicated this book, in part, to my daughter Scotland Rose. Brooke has been a constant in the lives of Scottie and I from the moment I told her I was expecting my first child, to the night I brought her into the world, to the current day. Her prayers and generosity of spirit have helped to carry me through some of the greatest heartaches a mother can endure – conditions not so different to the ones Brooke suffered from herself as a child. If I could add my own story to the ones she has written here, I would speak of the faithful prayers she has made for my Scottie, the love she showed me in the difficult seasons of motherhood, and the faithfulness of a friend who stays true even in the seasons of stretching when we see each other far too little. I rest easy in the knowledge that my daughter will always have a strong and faith-filled example to model herself upon and a loving friend who will always have our back.

I will also say that, as a friend who has been a part of her life for a large portion of the stories you are about to read, I could never speak highly enough of Brooke's deeply rooted commitment to doing what is right and honourable. She has allowed God to weave Himself securely into the tapestry of her life, forging an unbreakable relationship. Indeed, each time I have seen new attacks upon my own life, I have drawn much comfort over the years from her beautiful servant heart and courageous faith. I know, without a doubt, that treasure rests within these pages for those who are searching for that same comfort and courage that I have found. His faithfulness seeps through each and every word, His grace and forgiveness making all things new.

It has been one of my life's greatest honours to stand alongside Brooke as she has valiantly fought to be a pure vessel; pouring out her last drops in overwhelming circumstances, no answers and no choice but to put her hope and delight in Another. This is known as dying to self – it is also known as truly living.

I dare to believe that from this weighty book there will be miracles set in motion, relationships healed, hearts set on fire, and an overflow of blessings over the one who has painstakingly penned her journey onto these pages for us.

Bonnie Tan. Sydney, Australia

* * *

INTRODUCTION

Dear Reader,

Firstly, thank you for picking up this book. I am going to be completely honest from the outset and tell you that I did not want to write it. I did not want to discipline myself to carefully construct sentences or set time aside to pen some of my most raw life experiences. I did not want to revisit some memories or share the depth of those heartaches. I also did not want to acknowledge that in what I was able to learn from these moments, there would be a profound ripple effect in everything I would put my future hand and heart to. I stubbornly wrestled with the pull towards obedience when I felt this book regularly tugging at the seam of my conscience to be written. I think you get the point. I am either setting a very blunt and negative undertone to your reading experience, or perhaps (and hopefully more likely) I am stirring a little bit of curiosity in you, that in the forthcoming pages of this recount and collection of revelations there waits stories; stories that are brewing with rich revelation and the potential to unmask, perhaps, the mysterious face of God.

I hope it is okay with you, but I kind of just want to have a coffee (or a chai latte, or green tea – whatever tickles your fancy) and a conversation with you. I imagine stories are a lot more engaging when you are cosy and relaxed; when you are sitting across from your best friend in a café catching up on life, or cross legged on your bed listening to a grandparent reminisce about fond memories. I want you to feel like we have not seen each other in a while and I am simply filling you in on the things you missed. Like old friends.

I have been praying that if this snapshot of my life has anything of value worth hiding in the vault of your heart, it would be that there is a very kind and gracious King I have come to know. And He is extending His sweet invitation to you also, to come and know Him. He has let me sit at His feet and glean from His wisdom. He has lovingly corrected my sight when it has been off focus, and He has intimately spoken truth to my heart about His character in some of the most life-defining heartaches I have endured.

So friend, now that you are curious and comfortable, let's chat. These are the vulnerable pages of my diary, for your eyes only.

Love,

B xx

ROBUST
in love

I

DAY & NIGHT

What is BRAVERY?

When I was as young as three I can remember being fearful of the dark. Nothing scared me more than a dark bedroom, or going outside at night, or seeing the sun go down. I was what some might call a 'scaredy cat'. I did not like to be by myself, especially if it was dark and I could not sleep without at least the hallway light on. I almost always had nightmares. Diary, remember when Mum used to say I was an 'intense child'? Yep, this is why. I was gripped with fear and it made it impossible for me to sleep. Even right up until I was well into primary school I hated afternoons; afternoons meant that in just a few hours the sun would start to set and that meant night time. And night time meant nightmares.

Do you remember what my morning routine was? Mum would come and wake us kids up for school and my eyes would be almost glued shut with some kind of sticky substance. I know it is really gross but I used to have to put ointment on my eyelids every night; because I cried so much from the nightmares, by morning my eyes were not just puffy and red, they were sealed shut with gunk (sorry for the visual). I would have to spend at least twenty minutes of my morning cleaning my eyes with saline and then keep a damp facewasher across my face to help settle the puffiness. Some days, if I had not already told her in the night, Mum would ask what my dream was about. I would tell her between regular peeps from under the face washer; sometimes they were long descriptions and other times they were short. Either way, they were graphic and I could only retell them confidently because it was daytime and the shadows could not get to me (obviously). After that we would get dressed in uniforms. I would skip breakfast because I was too anxious to eat and then I would bite my nails the whole way to school. (Geez! That whole routine alone is contraception enough for me for at least the next thirty years!)

Hey Diary! Do you want to know a fun fact about me? Actually, I do not really know what element of it is fun; maybe it is just a fact. I am legally blind in my left eye. You would not be able to tell by looking at me, but if I am squinting or if I walk past you at the store, you can assume my left eye is to blame. I was not born blind though. I have scarring across my pupil that has blurred my vision. They say it is like if you repetitively scratched out a clear pane of glass, it would no longer be easy to see through. Such is the case with my eye. Growing up my eyes were the bane of my existence. Gosh they gave me grief! I was perfectly fine until we moved to Australia when I was three years old, and then I guess the heat caused a lot of problems for me. Not only did I start contracting eye infections but my body was covered in eczema. I was covered in scabs, in a constant state of irritation. My eyes were painfully sore and gooey all the time and I was too petrified to sleep. Combine that with a love of all things sport; a stubborn refusal to wear anything remotely girly; and frizz ball hair that would give Scary Spice a run for her money! Ergo INTENSE child.

I can remember Mum soaking me in oat baths. She used to lather me in my prescription eczema cream. I would cry as she tried to do it as quickly as possible because the sting was so horrible. She had to constantly remind me not to scratch and to wash my hands after touching anything and everything. My eyes were sensitive and my skin was sensitive and I was almost always in pain. From about three until I was just about to start high school, I was constantly in and out of doctors' and specialists' appointments. I routinely missed out on school to see specialists every month who tried to improve my sight. The best they could come up with was a complicated name for my condition, endless repeats for prescription medication, a recommendation for hard copies of any and all school work on an overhead, and a less than hopeful conclusion: Brooke will eventually go blind.

* * *

I think for most, from a young age, the first and most obvious example of love you glean from is that of your parents. And for my kindred spirits out there, it is undoubtedly the sternly protective love of Mufasa for a wildly playful Simba. Just for the record, *The Lion King* will always be the greatest Disney movie of all time!

I remember growing up always with a sense of a firm-footed, shatterproof kind of love from my parents. I am not sure that I always cared to return that kind of love as a young'un but I guess, now reflecting on it, I never doubted whether waking up in the morning I would have to prepare myself just in case Mum and Dad decided not to love me that day. It is crazy to think how much of what you see and feel as a child deeply roots itself in your foundational identity and becomes the soil from which you grow your little personality.

We did not grow up with a whole lot. In fact, neither did my parents, or my grandparents, and yep, their parents before them. So I guess you could say I am no stranger to struggle and grit. We had very humble beginnings. My mum fell pregnant at eighteen and had my older sister a handful of months after her nineteenth birthday. Then me at twenty-one, followed by my youngest sister at twenty-three. And then came the big move from a tiny town in Wellington, New Zealand, across the Tasman to Sydney, Australia. Mum talks about how she was heavily pregnant with my younger brother when we flew to Australia (in the middle of summer!) with only a bag of linen and $200 to our name … A family of almost six … *Whose brilliant idea was that?!*

I distinctly remember sharing a mattress with my siblings, each of us sticky and agitated with the heat, on the floor in a small room we shared with my parents. There was one window and one fan; you know the one I am talking about – the white 1.5 metre free standing ones that plugged into the wall. No sir, none of these fancy ceiling fans. We had the four speed buttons to control the intensity of cool wind this bad boy would blow in your desired direction. And yes, the knob on top to push down if you wanted the fan to oscillate its coveted wind supply, or to pull up if you wished it to remain still and blow directly ahead. My brother was a newborn and my sisters and I top and tailed a single mattress whilst my dad dampened towels and facewashers to keep us cool. The struggle was real. I can still hear the funny noises my siblings and I would sing into the fan as it blowed and distorted our voices. (You are lying if you say that even now as a grown up, you would not immediately sing into a fan for entertainment if the opportunity presented itself.)

It was at least six months before our family graduated from the small confines of that room and managed to move into our own place – riddled with cockroaches and void of furniture – where we lived off canned Irish stew and scotch fingers. Like I said, humble.

STALKING SHADOWS

Have you ever had a dream that felt so real that when you woke up you were either in a pool of sweat or your heart was racing or you realised you had been crying in your sleep? A dream that felt so real that it kind of threw you off for the rest of your day as you found yourself trying to remember all the details of the dream and figure out what it meant. Personally I hate those dreams. I have only ever had this happen to me a handful of times, but it has been the same dream. I used to have all the standard nightmares when I was younger. There is the 'someone breaking into the house' dream; the 'parents die in a car crash' dream; the 'little brother gets kidnapped by butchers' dream; the 'Cruella de Vil standing over my bed watching me sleep' dream; the 'creepy guy living under my bed' dream etc. But there was one dream I would have that was the scariest of all my nightmares. This dream would have me trembling in my parents' bed with fear. I would cry uncontrollably; in part because I did not know what it meant but mostly because I could not forget what I saw. I learned fear has a way of etching images into your memory that even years later have the ability to slip a cold bony hand over your mouth and whisper in your ear, "Don't make a sound …"

Cry is his name. That is the guy who stalked my dreams. What a fitting name, hey? Because he always made me cry. He was a slender man. His cheeks were gaunt and his eyes were dark with heavy eyeliner. He had pasty white skin and bleached hair spiked with sharp intent. His ears were metallically lined with rows of piercings and he had a black teardrop tattoo under his right eye. Cry wore heavy boots and dragged a chain behind him. In my dream I was the only person who could see him, but the most chilling thing was that I was also the only person who could hear him. And that was worse. He never said a word to me. He would just let me know he was coming because I could hear the scuff of his boots and the scratch of his chain along the ground. He watched me everywhere I went and he always brought dark storm clouds with him.

In my dream we were at a carnival and the sky had turned black. I knew he was coming and I was desperately trying to find my family members so we could leave. The crowds were scurrying now because lightning had started to flash. Mothers were pulling their whining toddlers away from the lines for their favourite rides as the game stallholders were pleading with patrons to 'step on up and beat the highest score' for the coveted stuffed toy. The colourful lights flickered above clown heads moving from side to side. The wind picked up and whipped the flags above the tent. And I hurried through the masses looking for my big sister.

Thunder cracked with an amplified roar and we all jumped with fright. I could hear the chain dragging and the footsteps coming but I could not see him anywhere. I spun around scanning the crowd with a rapidly beating chest. People rushed in all directions collecting belongings and children, seeking shelter from the brewing storm. My eyes darted frantically from face to face. Then I locked eyes with a face that froze me still.

There he was, standing but ten metres from me in front of a flapping circus tent.

He did not walk towards me. He did not say anything to me.

He just stared at me.

He did not blink and I did not breathe. The corners of his cracked lips curved into a taunting smile and revealed sharpened teeth and a dark tongue. His bony fingers and black varnished nails suspended something familiar next to his face. I felt my bare neck. There in his grasp he dangled my necklace; a family heirloom passed down to me from my nana.

I never know what happens next, because the four times I have had this exact dream, I wake up full of fear and rush to my mum's room to cry. I cry hysterically, because no one scares me as much as he does. My mum lets me climb into her bed and she holds my hand and prays over me and then we ask for God's peace to give me rest. I have always stayed lying in my mum's bed, gripping her arm and staring alert at the bedroom door. If it is open, I watch the hallway for shadows. If it is closed,

I watch the handle for movement and routinely check the corners of the room for his figure. At least I used to. It has probably been five or so years since he last appeared.

I remember some nights having bad dreams and waking up suddenly. My heart would be beating super fast and my eyes were already flooded with tears. Some nights I would be paralysed with fear and stiff in my bed. Other nights I would call out to my parents. Occasionally, I would get up and make a run for it to their bedroom. I do not know what is it about staircases but I swear they increase the fear factor by roughly 2572%. I hated running past the stairs. I always thought Cry would be waiting at the foot of the stairs for me or that he would be crouching on the half way landing. Isn't it ironic that being petrified of the dark made me too scared to get up and switch on the light? So I would run as quickly as I could to my mum and just hope that the shadows could not catch me in the hallway before I made it to safety.

One of the most consistent things my parents made me do when I could not sleep was read my Bible. They would tell me to read it until I fell asleep. Honestly, I thought this was funny because when you are young, reading the Bible is boring so it always worked like a charm! Before I knew it I was counting sheep! Nights in our house were … interesting.

Days were much more exciting because there was always a spirit of generosity about the way my parents governed our possessions. And our home was always open. We had a family friend stay with us for a period of time who we affectionately called *Nana Rachel*. I still do not really know the full story of how she came to live with us but the standard my parents had set was that we were to be respectful and kind anyway. Nana Rachel knitted us beanies and we would often pray for her granddaughters who were navigating their teens. She scared me a little. She used to play this mean joke on poor unsuspecting four-year-old me: I would walk past her, minding my own business, and she would seize the opportune moment to suddenly push her dentures out of her mouth in a vomit like fashion and then lean back in her chair and wheeze with laughter at my frightened reaction. Not cool Nana Rachel, not cool.

Sometimes she would let me help her roll cigarettes. She would lay a sheet in front of me and a sheet in front of her before distributing the perfect amount of tobacco onto the rolling papers with her yellow stained fingertips. And then she slowly showed me how to secure the bud and roll before licking the excess overlap to seal it. I remember, as little as I was, just sensing that Nana Rachel did not have a lot of people loving her. She did not have a whole lot of people being generous with their time or words or hospitality. And here we were, I do not think even remotely related, and not bearing much to offer except that we had this willingness to just love her anyway. Some traumatic things had been happening with her granddaughter and she leant on my parents for encouragement and reassurance. And even prayer. I do not remember her ever coming to church with us, or reading her Bible, but she knew she could ask us to pray. And she knew we would love her through her pain.

Growing up, my parents wasted no time raising us kids to live lives that served others. If you thought our beginnings were humble … well, every Saturday we would all trek forty minutes or so into Redfern. There was a section of this Sydney suburb known as 'The Block', densely populated by Aboriginal peoples of Australia and unfortunately home to a poverty-stricken demographic in the heart of one of the world's most thriving cities (go figure!). It had a reputation (and still does to this day) of being one of the roughest neighbourhoods in Sydney. And the tension in this neighbourhood was heightened towards outsiders because of lingering prejudices as the indigenous Australians were oppressed for many, many years due to colonisation. So, in short, my parents decided it was a good idea for us to go into that neighbourhood every week and run a kids' program. In case you are still not tracking with me, these residents are not always the most welcoming of outsiders and you do not just waltz on into their block with no indigenous blood and run a program for their children. But we did it. And we did it faithfully for a few years.

One of my earliest memories of The Block was our family in the car – it was evening and we took a drive through this segregated grid, I guess to get familiar with the area. There were people congregated around fires, and young snot-strewn faces were running barefoot on roads covered with shattered glass. I saw old men obnoxiously slurring colourful language between sips from a firmly gripped brown paper bag. I remember hearing my parents praying over The Block as we drove through it, with the locals eye-balling our car. At a particular cross-section we had rolled to a stop and to the right there was a small park with two worn out swing sets. It was a poorly lit section of The Block but I clearly remember seeing a pregnant teenage girl inserting a needle into her belly. My parents recall stories of being threatened with being stabbed and crazy things alike. I do not think you need any more descriptive scenarios to be convinced it was a dangerous place to be. It was a dangerous place to bring your young family. It was a dangerous place to bring love and kindness to people who had been starved of it.

I can remember Mum would steward a tight budget to feed these kids every week. We would provide them with lunch and play games and sport, and watch movies with them. We took them to Wonderland (at the time the greatest theme park in Western Sydney) and eventually we earned the respect of the elders in The Block. There were times my mum was emotional because these kids were in such great need; we were giving them maybe their only decent meal for the week and yet she was struggling to buy essentials for her own kids. Some days my sister and I went to school with butter on bread or no breakfast because it was always a stretch. And we had Christmases where my parents could only afford to buy us glow sticks from the discount store as presents. But what these kids sorely lacked that we had an abundance of, was love.

It was not just us who had humble beginnings; in fact, my parents had upbringings that never even promised them a future outside of destructively repetitive cycles. My dad is the product of a broken home. He never got an education past the 8th or 9th grade before he was forced to leave school and join the workforce. His parents had divorced and he had younger siblings to help care for when his mum abandoned them to start a new life and family. He inevitably fell into the party and drug scene, developing a reputation established by bloodshot eyes and top shelf spirits. He was the embodiment of the term 'black sheep of the family'.

My mum is the namesake of a deceased older sister. I know, it is creepy right? She was also subjected to the predatory, sexually abusive hands of her father for many years. She too sought pain relief from the party, drug and alcohol scene. When I think about their backgrounds, I can't ignore that miracles exist if these two became the parents that raised me. The truth is, that statistically speaking, I should not be here. My family should not be here. Mum should be in an abusive relationship, or have aborted every foetus she carried, or become a sex offender herself, or even taken her own life. My dad should be a drug-dealer, or in prison, or divorced, or quite possibly dead by now. Their marriage surely should not have survived to this point. Our family should not be together … or so they say.

As long as I have been alive my parents have always been two of the strongest, most faith-filled, trust-Jesus-no-matter-what kind of people in my life. I know for a fact that any ounce of resilience I have has been a trait I learned from them. Their marriage and their faith stance are often admired for their robust stature. They wear resilience like a suit of armour and they are seldom found in the battlefield of life without it, side by side. Trench buddies, you could say. Do I think it is by chance that they have persevered through trying times and hardship and years of familiarity, yet remain standing? Nope. Not a chance. They have navigated some very humble origins and protected their resolve to honour God and their commitment to each other before, during and after the storms of life.

Are there enough words to esteem and honour people as sacrificial as my parents? I do not know if there ever will be. If there is anything their lives of love have taught me, it is that day and night force you to face different things. But the one consistent thing they hold onto is that their faith sustains them, and our lives and journey as a family, thus far, are proof of that.

Love,

B xx

PS Diary, when I grow up I want to have a faith walk like theirs. It is *brave* and *inspirational* from every angle.

II

STAY WITH ME

Dear Diary,

Is BRAVERY an action, attitude or attribute?

Do you want to hear about the crappiest year of my life? It is a really funny story, I promise (although you might want to have a pocket pack of tissues handy just in case). It is funny to me now, because looking back I can see how necessary it was for me to go through the ridiculous hardships that year presented me.

Picture this, right? It is Christmas Eve 2012; there is joy and excitement in the air. The tree is over-decorated with lights and tinsel. Only the peppermint candy canes are left dangling on the tree because my siblings and I have been sneakily stealing the rainbow ones and eating them over the past few weeks. There is an abundance of wrapped gifts of all sizes footing the tree and everyone is blasting Mariah Carey's 'All I want for Christmas' in their homes, cars and stores. The atmosphere is full of giddy, childlike anticipation because soon and very soon we will be wide-eyed in joy-filled surprise at the gifts we receive (even though we specifically requested them and dropped hints like bombshells for months in the lead up).

On this magical day I walk into my parents' bedroom and find my mum sitting on her bed puffy-eyed and sniffling with tear-streaked cheeks. Suddenly Mariah falls silent. And now suspense hangs in the air because when Mama cries something is very wrong.

TEARS

I have always thought my mum was a pretty crier. I know, it is random, but ask any female and you will come to understand that pretty criers are a real thing, as real as ugly criers. I would like to say that I fall into the same category as my mum but who am I kidding? My top lip swells like I was stung by a bee, snot runs more free-flowing than a tap and my morning-after eyes earned me the nickname Puff Daddy … (whatever, I do not want to talk about it). Anyway, back to my mum.

Growing up we saw Mum cry regularly. No, she was not emotionally unstable. She would simply let her tears fall freely whenever she was worshipping in church. If there is anything I have learned from observing my mum in worship, it is that she is not afraid to be vulnerable before her King. It is really beautiful.

My mum has always said that I was a very intense child. I was keenly observant, frustratingly stubborn and unapologetically independent. I knew what I liked and knew even better what I did not like. She will tell you that I was confidently intelligent, sarcastically outspoken and (in her words) annoyingly good at a lot of things. She will also then leave a pregnant pause – just enough to catch your curious gaze – and tell you that from a very young age, I was spiritually aware. That even as young as three I was unmistakably sensitive to the Spirit. Maybe overcoming nightmares and health struggles are predictive of greater battles waiting ahead.

That being said, when I walked in to find my mum crying, immediately my spirit knew there was a depth of sorrow from which her tears had been drawn and I sensed a very real pain seeped from her water-logged eyes. When I was little I watched my mum cry in worship without understanding why; but somehow I knew that she was not crying because she was upset or hurt. I would watch her raise her hands and tilt her head upward to sing and I watched her tears trickle from beneath gently rested eyelids. I watched this every week at church; I almost knew exactly when the first tear would appear – worship set song one, build to bridge and 3, 2, 1 – right on cue.

I know that as a young'un you do not always have the ability to articulate comfort in a tactful manner; but I realise you do not have to teach a child how to comfort with action. It comes very naturally. Touch is immensely effective. While I am certain there is a lengthy and very interesting scientific study that explains this sensory property, I think simply put, touch connects our spirit men. So, on the handful of occasions I was brave enough to interrupt her worship, I would stand next to Mum and hold her hand.

I circled her bed and came beside her to ask what was wrong. Like all strong mothers, she wiped her tears and said, "It's ok, I'll tell you later," and we hugged. The stubborn sixteen-year-old side of me wanted to challenge her to tell me now, but the spiritually sensitive side of me knew I should probably let my mum have this moment. And whilst we are on the topic of the phenomenal woman she is, I may as well reassure you that she definitely did tell me and my siblings what was happening. My mama is a woman of her word. But it would not be for another two days, so that we could enjoy Christmas. Yep, she is strong and incredible.

It was Boxing Day and my parents sat us kids down to explain why Mum was crying. We all sat fairly close to each other, I guess for reassurance that we as the kids could be collectively strong for Mum and Dad if this news was really bad. Mum told us that Grandad might be going back to prison. He was being held and there was an upcoming trial to determine the truth and the next twenty or so years of his life. Then, accompanied by gushing tears, her wounds ripped raw as she explained that her father had been accused of child molestation. Again.

* * *

A few weeks later I was on an annual summer camp with my

church youth group. It was my last year as a student and I was expectant that it would be the best one yet. I remember being in one of the camp night rallies and having a moment with Jesus in worship where I was thinking about my year ahead. *Okay God, I'm in year 12. We have got HSC … What university should I apply for? How many awards am I going to get at the presentation ceremony? What Bible reading plan should I start next? Ahem? Hello?*

I wish I could tell you that He answered so clearly all of the questions I shot at Him. But He did not. Instead I felt an ever so gentle scribble on my heart followed by a whisper, "Stay with me." That was it: *stay with me.* I sort of chuckled to myself and replied, "C'mon God, of course I'll stay with you."

And just like that the punches came rolling in; life fired shots as brutally destructive as a flock of seagulls flying overhead (with diarrhoea). Welcome to the crappiest year of my life.

TALES

Grandad went to trial and he pleaded guilty to all charges brought against him. He confessed to graphically horrific allegations and like most repeat offenders, attempted to justify his actions by deflecting blame and responsibility onto the victim. I think while we are here I will join some dots for you. My first few years of life in New Zealand included some visits to prison to see my Grandad. I guess, when this is the way to view the extent of his involvement in my childhood, it is easy to be emotionally detached. Our family's seemingly unwise move from New Zealand to Australia and the subsequent years of struggle as a young family was actually a well-thought-through decision my parents made in order that my siblings and I could grow up in an environment free of his prowling lust-filled eyes. And yes, you read correctly – *repeat offender.* He sexually abused my mum for a gross proportion of her childhood, robbing her innocence and purity. Defiling her soul and violating her body. Greedily salivating at her virgin trust and grating away at her self-worth. So now my mama's tears began swirling from a deep, deep reserve.

My parents grew up rough, and their pre-Jesus lives were dominated by the lure of drug and alcohol abuse. My mum says the pain of reliving the traumatic things done to her as a child, even after becoming a Christian and receiving healing, was enough to push her right back into drinking. In fact, she had planned to binge the very week my siblings and I were away on summer camp. Remember when I said Mum would cry in worship? One day I asked her why she always cried in church and she told me that her tears were not sadness. They were gratitude. They were tears of remembrance because she was broken and dirty and had had a tarnished start to life. But when she met Jesus He lovingly washed over her like a waterfall and began mending all the brokenness. He let her heal from the wounds wearing away at the remains of her heart and He spoke truth to her about His goodness. He helped her forgive, sincerely. And then He started letting her dream big dreams about her future and her family.

If I am being honest, watching my mum re-live this hurt brewed a red-hot hate in me toward my Grandad. I hated him. Not even strongly disliked, but proper hated. To the extent that if he was going to rot in prison for the rest of his life, I would be a hundred percent OK with that. Or if he got released early on parole, but due to some unfortunate mistiming was hit by a bus and died on the spot, I would not have batted an eyelid. In fact, I may have hi-fived the bus driver if that ever happened. That is how ugly my hate was for him. And yet at the peak of my hatred I can remember two very distinct squirming moments. My mum (of all people) in her profound wisdom hit me up one day and taught me (as she did with all of my siblings) that *forgiveness* is always a must. It is compulsory.

"Brooke, you don't get to choose to forgive someone or not because you constantly need God's forgiveness for yourself." (Trust is optional, and that part you can hold out on for as long as you need to, until you can wisely discern whether it can be extended or not).

The second thing that caused me to squirm was a simple

question; a question that came in the form of a gentle internal whisper, "Brookie, is this what robust love looks like?"

Flip. Heart check.

A few months later I was well into my HSC studies. Like most of my peers, the pressure was starting to build up and could be credited for sleepless nights, worrisome conversations, nervous energy and more hours logged in library study than any of us would care to admit. Year 12 is no joke. But the promise of freedom from the dreaded school gates for the rest of our lives was more than enough incentive to persevere through. So here we were a few weeks out from HSC trial examinations and our family received a letter in the mail. We had had a series of open home inspections for potential buyers and this letter was to notify us that the house we lived in had been sold, and we had thirty days to move out.

This is the part where, if I was telling you in person, I would laugh hysterically as I watched your face as you desperately searched my eyes for a glimpse of reassurance that this letter was not as unsettling as it would be in a movie. And if I was not laughing hysterically, I would probably tell you as I sobbed uncontrollably – there is really no in between. This point of our lives was so ridiculous it may as well have been an epic cinematic drama. Surely it could not have been real life? Well, we were not in a movie but it sure was the beginning of a wild four-and-a-half-month journey of homelessness. Yeah. We were homeless. I was homeless throughout my entire HSC trial exams, my HSC prep and the entire first week of my proper HSC exams. Yikes. I will just give you a moment to pick your jaw up off the floor.

How does a family of six navigate not having a home? Well, you throw all your belongings into storage; pack an overnight bag; divide yourselves between family and friends; and trust God for a miracle. I wish I could say it was a breeze finding a new home. I wish I could say that we did not endure complications within our complications. But this story would be super boring if not and why else would God feel the need to give me a three word heads up before my year unfolded? *Stay with Me.*

I just want to clarify that we did not spend any nights on the street. I say homeless because we were home-less. We went to open home inspection after open home inspection, sometimes two or three a day. We would even split up and my sisters and I would view a house whilst my parents simultaneously viewed another. And we were desperately praying that our applications would be approved. I cannot even recall the number of rejections we got, but let's just say it was four and a half months' worth before we got a miracle. During this time my sisters and I were separated from my parents and brother. They were fortunate enough to stay with some beautiful family friends for the entire time we were without a place of our own. My sisters and I on the other hand couch-hopped. We lived out of duffle bags and packed up and moved every few weeks to stay temporarily with generous friends who took turns opening their homes to us. I counted five moves.

And just to add insult to injury, during this time my Dad got seriously injured whilst doing a landscaping job and wound up in hospital, needing surgery followed by an extensive recovery period before he could return to any labour-intensive work. So now we were down to my mum's income. And then Mum's hours at work got cut from five days to three. So now we were stuck. How does that look on an application? As a parent, how do you cope with the cloud of failure already weighing on you that you can't put a roof over your children's head? And then how do you accept the financial help offered by your eldest daughter's full time wage out of her generous heart? How do you hang onto your faith when it seems like the hole is only getting deeper?

Let's add a bit more salt to the wound, shall we? Have you ever had a bad day and thought it could not get any worse and then almost as if the universe heard your cute little thought, it throws another spanner into the works just to laugh at you like an amateur skater constantly fumbling on ice? Yeah, well we had two cars. It worked out well because it meant my sisters and I had one to use for our various temporary addresses and my parents had one also. But our cars did the good ol' tag team and decided they were not going to work for us anymore. Of course. (I was so sure that ridiculous storylines like this only happen in Hollywood but apparently not.) I do not know what it is about car troubles, but if you ever want to feel lower than low, wait for the day your car decides not to work for you and then you will feel like a total loser.

I remember anxiety gripping me around the neck. I was so anxious that I was scared to breathe. I had a bag for my books and a bag for my clothes. I had a brave face for school but I was trembling under the surface. *Brooke, hold it together, just get through this class. Brooke don't let anyone see you cry, you don't want rumours spreading that you are homeless. Brooke, you can't apply for university, you don't even have a home address. Brooke, it looks like you need extensions on all your final assessments. Tough luck, you worked so hard but now your whole life is falling apart.*

God where are you? You told me to stay! And I am here! But where are You?

I persisted through my studies with a bucket load of grit. I had emotional breakdowns every week and boiled with frustration at peers who would whine and complain about how stressful their lives were trying to juggle their homework while keeping up with their favourite Netflix series. But here I was struggling to get my final assessments completed on time because from week to week I was not certain I even had a place to live. I was not even living with my parents. All sense of security was violently shaken. The anxiety overcame me when I started to notice my hard-earned ranks dropping in some of my strongest subjects. And if I can be completely honest, I felt like a total failure when I did not receive a single academic achievement award at the end-of-year presentation ceremony. Not a single award. For as long as I can remember, every year I have been recognised for outstanding academic achievements; except for the year that counted the most. What a failure. I missed out on applying for university because my biggest priority was applying for tenancy in a home; any home! I often broke down with waves of self-doubt that I could even get the ATAR I had hoped for; so in an effort to ease the blow, I secretly lowered my expectations as a personal allowance for my home situation (or lack thereof). When I finally received the letter post HSC with my results, I cried for a couple of hours. You can definitely ask my parents to verify how disappointed I was for not reaching the high achiever bench mark I had set for myself. Looking back now I can see how silly it was because I still scored comparatively with the studious front-runners of my cohort. But at the time, the personal blow to my self-esteem was a total KO and I was definitely not OK.

I had every reason to walk away from God. In fact, that is exactly what I wanted to do. This faith my parents clung to with every stride was not looking like a promising deal to me. My mum will testify that I became a very difficult seventeen-year-old. I had grown bored of attending youth group on a weekly basis. I did not see the point in guarding my heart and so I grew a very unhealthy emotional attachment to a boy whom I was never supposed to. A rebellious attitude began to develop within me, and with it came an appetite for the clubbing scene; I became altogether insecure in my identity. Thank God Mum could see how insecure I had become! Thank God she did everything to pull out the secure woman she knew I could be. She grounded me from posting selfies on social media. Yup. She is ruthless like that. But it was the best thing she could have ever done for me. My feed was all about me and the likes and comments became my source of value. My mum forced me to find my true identity and become a woman of substance. The tactic may have been unconventional at the time and I was definitely not a fan of having character built into me, but Diary, I might just pocket this form of refinement for my future daughter. It did me a world of good. Thanks Mum!

I can remember the day I got the call that we were approved for a house. I remember sitting at a dining room table with my friend Stephy as we studied for our upcoming PDHPE exam. It was the first week of proper HSC exams and tensions were running high. I had already sat two out of three exams scheduled on my timetable for that week and was feeling the urgency to cram study notes at all hours of the day. My phone rang, interrupting our focussed study and I answered rather irritated. My big sister's voice delivered the news we had been waiting almost five long months to hear, "We got the house!" There is not a decibel reading that could match the squeal of joy that left my mouth. Followed by jumping and victory dancing I am not too sure I care to describe, because I know you will judge me. *What a relief! Thank you Jesus!*

I sat my PE exam that Friday and we moved into our new house the very next day. I know, how backwards to think that moving house smack bang in the middle of my HSC exams would actually be the highlight of my year! I guess all that frequent moving around had made me super adaptable to changing conditions, hey? It was preparing me to see some life interruptions as divine interventions. If that whisper had elaborated a little, at the start of the year, and told me that I would be jumping with joy because of a miracle, it all would have made a bit more sense. It certainly would have saved me a lot of tears and bratty moments of arguing with God about why such painful things were happening to us. But then I do not think I would have been able to acknowledge His hand of favour when the miracle eventually did come.

In a strange way it reminds me of when I used to be obsessed with Roald Dahl. He was hands down my favourite author when I was in primary school. As a keen little learner and occasional creative writer, I would always be drawn deep into this imaginative experience whenever I read his books. When it came to library time every week I was the eager kid prepared with library bag and on a mission to hunt down the next book to devour. I knew exactly where to find Mr Dahl's books and I was guilty of re-borrowing his novels back to back. I derived great enjoyment from his most popular reads like *Charlie and the Chocolate Factory*, *Fantastic Mr Fox*, *The Twits*, *James and the Giant Peach*, *The BFG,* and if you were really loyal you read *Charlie and the Glass Elevator.* I think you can tell I am a fan; I read these books over and over again. It crushed me to learn of his passing, but I held a profound respect for Dahl's descriptive writing as I farewelled hopes of ever shaking the hand of such a talented scribe. I found that I trusted his narration even in the most gripping chapters of his novels. I always found sweet comfort in his writing because, although I was fully engrossed in the complicated nature of that particular chapter, I trusted that the author knew how to perfectly round off the novel and give me a satisfactory ending. I do not know how else to explain it, but I just knew. I just trusted him.

Stay. With. Me. These were the words the Ultimate Author scribed on my heart at the beginning of an intense year that would see me squirm and squeal. It saw me question every good thing about my God's character. I struggled to trust His narration of my story because I was too caught up in surviving the complicated chapters. I think I have realised there is much to be said of someone who can remain standing. Maybe bravery gives us 'staying power', the type of resilience that eventually gets to squeal with joy. Diary, I might have discovered that Mum and Dad's example of faith is only enough for me to follow. But to stay? I think that kind of faith and bravery has to be my own.

My resolve is He is good. He is faithful. And He is true to His Word.

So I am staying with Him.

Love,

B xx

III

ROSE–ILIENCE

Is BRAVERY spontaneous or premeditated?

Have you ever caught yourself admiring the striking beauty of a single stem rose? It is delicate and dangerous all at once; its velvet petals of deep red are contrasted by the threatening thorns staggered along its stem. Even when dried out, the rose is simply stunning to study. Isn't it a captivating thought that something so mesmerisingly rich in beauty can also be devastatingly harmful if not handled with caution? Roses are unmistakable icons of love, passion and beauty, but there is also a secret strength. The thorns are protective barriers and represent an acknowledgment of potential harm; maybe from thieves that seek to tamper with the rose's unmatched beauty. What a juxtaposition: *Strength* and *Vulnerability*.

I want to introduce you to a real life rose. She is my formidably beautiful big sister. She has the most contagious smile you have ever seen. Apart from the fact that she was blessed with perfectly aligned pearly whites, her smile is the kind that encourages her entire face to join in the celebration. Her cheek bones pop and her brows rise ever so slightly and her eyes squint just enough to reveal tiny dimples on either side of her temple. Simply put, she is stunning. Now when you witness this smile in real life, it is only human to be thinking that you want to quickly find something you do not like about her smile (because as if someone could be that beautiful) but then she would say something mountainously encouraging and you would be diffused. Then watching her from a distance you may think you could catch her off guard being nasty, but instead she would most likely have bought you a thoughtful little gift or paid for your lunch, and once again you would be left scratching your head, wondering how someone could outdo their own physical beauty with the tenderness of their generous heart. That is my sister. A rose.

My sister is also a fighter. She has an unrelenting strong side – the true definition of an eldest sibling. I remarked of her in my speech at her 21st birthday that, "She never had to be taught how to be a big sister, she just is." And no truer statement could have ever been made. She is dangerously protective of her family, in particular her siblings. Beautiful to look at, yes, but do wrong by her family and I would suggest you make the most of the 2.5 second head start she gives you to run as fast as your little legs will go, before she hunts you down with the ferocity of a lioness protecting her cubs. "Don't mess with my family," she has always said. Yep, that's my sister.

Growing up, of course, she was the first to get a part time job and the first to get her licence. She was also always the first to get into trouble when I and my younger siblings ran wild. My big sister loved being generous; especially with gift giving. That's where she and I are different. She would start compiling her Christmas shopping list in September and start purchasing in October (what a show off). She would buy lots and lots of little gifts and then usually one bigger, more expensive gift. And she got just as excited to see you open them as you were to receive them. Generous with her time, she always made it a priority to be on call for her family. I remember her saying once that her only motivation for getting her licence was so she could drive the forty minutes or more to visit our cousins more regularly and to be able to bring them to church if they ever wanted to come. Every year she would offer to pay for them to attend camps and events and always made it clear that she valued her family more than anything. She definitely stood in the gap for us siblings. There were many occasions that she copped the overall blame as the eldest child for our collectively irresponsible actions. In hindsight, we were quite a mischievous bunch, and she should not have backed us, but we have some incredibly hilarious memories and it is all thanks to her. She is my favourite big sister (relax, she is also my only big sister). She is a rose.

GRACE FOR GRIT

The Rose has always been someone I look up to. She carries herself gracefully and loves with ease. I have always admired her willingness to do hard things. She has made some hard calls. And been a sturdy backbone when our family has been shaken.

We were preparing for a family trip to Hawaii a few years back as it had always been a destination to check off the family bucket list. It promised to be the greatest two weeks of our lives, enjoying all the perks the island has to offer. We had lined up all the best touristy things to do and see and we were extra excited because Mum and Dad were renewing their vows in celebration of twenty years of marriage.

I do not know how to say this tactfully, but we hated it. Not because the beaches and the food and shopping did not live up to our expectations, but because the day we flew out of Sydney the ugliest curve ball was thrown our way.

The tension at the kitchen table was so thick. There were tears and there was very little eye contact. The hurt was real. The betrayal was real. The fear was real. There are few feelings in life that are worse than fearing your parents' divorce. It is ugly. There was so much going on. There was the feeling of shock at what we had just learned; the anger that raged while not understanding why it had happened; the disappointment that now we could not enjoy our holiday. And then the worst of it all, "Are Mum and Dad going to stay married?"

When Mum and Dad got married they made a vow before God to love each other till death. They were committed to defying odds and roughing the trenches. They were choosing each other over the millions of other candidates this world offered. They were exclusively merging two souls into one. But that morning shook the foundations of these vows.

I woke up excited to experience our first family holiday in Hawaii with eager anticipation. What would it look like? What would it smell like? Where would we make the best memories? What hilarious holiday adventure stories would we return home with? These were all questions I was excited to know the answers to, but they were abruptly hushed when I overheard arguing form behind my parents' bedroom door. "C'mon guys," I initially thought to myself, "Don't start our trip on a bad note." I quietly crept out of my room, careful not to wake my younger sister and tiptoed to the hallway to listen in. Mum had that tone, the tone that demanded answers. Dad had sort of a sheepish response. He was telling her to calm down, but I could tell it was only frustrating her more. My mum was asking *why*, asking questions about *her*. Who was this 'her'? Did I know 'her'? Mum wanted to know why Dad had pictures of her on his phone. She wanted to know why Dad thought he could explain it away in two sentences. From what I could make out, these pictures were not of my mum and they certainly were not innocent photos that escaped suspicion. My heart dropped. "Oh God, please no no no! Please don't let this be true!"

DADDY'S LITTLE GIRL

I grew up a die-hard Daddy's girl. He was simply my favourite person in the world. We liked the same things and I prided myself on the closeness I had with my dad. My siblings joked for years that I was his favourite child (just for the record he never denied it). We loved sport and spicy food. We trained together and we shared an unhealthy addiction to hats and shoes. If there was something he was to teach us, I wanted to be the first to perfect it; whether it was folding a paper plane or learning our native tongue or refining a clean 6 o'clock pass. I used to want to play the drums and then the guitar and then the keyboard. He taught me what he knew and I picked it up quickly before I got bored and found the next thing to be good at. I discovered I was kind of good at art and creative writing, so he let me paint in the garage and was usually the first person I shared my writings with. If he was watching a game, I sat there too and listened to him passionately support his team. When I had touch footy tournaments or Oz-tag games I did not mind if no one else supported me, as long as he did, and as long as I could show him a medal or trophy or brag about a try or set up.

I remember he went through a phase where he was really into drinking grapefruit juice, which was nothing like the cordial we grew up on. None of my siblings took a liking to it and to be perfectly honest, I thought it tasted pretty gross. But because Dad liked it, I drank it until I liked it; just so I could be like him. When I was in my first year of high school and topping my grade in English, we had to write and present about the person who inspired us the most. You guessed it, I chose my dad. When Dad was playing bass for church, I would stay awake every Wednesday night until he got back from rehearsals. If I had to choose between doing something girlie with my mum and sisters or doing something sporty with my dad and brother, I chose the latter.

When I was well into my adolescent years and fighting to be an independent woman who did not need to answer to my mother anymore, Dad was usually the middle man in the thick of my arguments. I was a brat (Mum, I am really sorry for all of that!) and Dad played peacekeeper and mediator between the two most stubborn people in the house. He used to say to me all the time that I was just like my mother and that is why we bumped heads, but I was not having a bar of it. I wanted him to pick my side every single time (which was super unfair, because as I said, I was a brat). If my mum asked me to do something I would roll my eyes, but if Dad asked me to do the same thing, homeboy never had to ask me twice! If my mum did not approve of an outfit, I sulked. But if my dad did not approve, obviously it was for a reason and I was inclined to take it on board. If Mum said no to something, I went to Dad because nine times out of ten I got the opposite answer. For me, growing up my dad could do no wrong in my eyes. He was the strongest man I knew. He was fun and hip and made us laugh all the time. He was unapologetically passionate and was often mistaken for our brother. Most of our friends had a crush on him, and none of the guys made direct eye contact with him. And to top it all off, he was pierced and tattooed and had a mysteriously dark past he would not spend a whole lot of time sharing with us.

My dad was cool. And everyone knew it. He would pick us up from school blasting Bob Marley, hanging a tatted arm out the window. He did not even go by his given name. He sort of just decided one day to go by something different and no one challenged him. He was the cool uncle all my cousins respected. They loved his style and his energy. Dad never seemed like he was trying hard. He just had a natural swag and people gravitated towards him. And amid all of that seemingly reckless freedom, he was loyal to my mum. He was the protector of our family. I was going to marry someone just like my dad one day. He was my hero.

But suddenly the occupant of my highest pedestal was in the interrogation room and I was not confident his alibi would check out. *How did we get here? Did my dad really betray my mum? Why? Why did he do that? Why didn't he think of us? Were we not enough for him? Was I not a good enough daughter that in the moments he could have chosen us over 'her', he chose outside of his flesh and blood? When did he become distant from us? Did we refuse to love him and force him to drift?* As far as I was concerned, my dad did not just hurt my mum, he directly hurt me. I am the product of them both. I am part of him. And now I had just learned that it was not enough for him to pause and consider how his actions might just sever our relationship beyond mending. My whole life I just wanted to be his girl. I just wanted him to notice me and approve of me. I wanted him to choose me. And in one split second, even as his child, I was not enough to keep him here with us, whole-heartedly. He may have been present physically, but we had had no idea his mind and heart had wandered away. Did my dad just reject us for something that pleased his eyes? He did not think of my mum. He did not think of our family. He did not think of me. This was a heartbreaking reality: my hero betrayed my mum. It was as simple and as complex as that. I was destroyed.

When we sat at the table that morning, I could not look at him. I could not stand the fact that he was breathing and sitting right next to me. I hated him. In that moment I hated him. And I am ashamed to admit that.

My brave big sister broke the silence with a chin quiver and said, "I love you all. Our family has been through heaps of hard stuff, but we have always come out stronger. We are founded on God and I believe He is going to get us through this. Mum and Dad, I love you but we are not splitting. Divorce is not an option. Us kids love you both! We are staying together!" And just like that she boldly reminded our family of who we are and why we fight for each other. She thwarted the seeds of doubt that we could overcome this giant hurdle. She bravely declared that she was going to fight for us and enlisted the rest of us to get on the same page. It took every ounce of strength in her. She fought to speak through her heavy-hearted tears and shaky voice, but she had all the conviction she needed. And although we knew there was rough terrain ahead, our Rose was going to lead with confidence.

The flight to Hawaii was the first time us kids ever witnessed my mum resort to the bottle to numb the pain. And that was hard. I am not exaggerating when I say that my big sister was the ultimate damage control officer. She played the role of Mum and Dad for the best part of a year after that heart-wrenching morning. She played referee when they fought. She played taxi driver when we could not stand to be around them. She played responsible adult when my parents bickered from a place of bitter hurt. I remember there was a night she had gone out to celebrate a friends' birthday and my younger siblings and I were at home. Mum and Dad got into a heated discussion and it boomed thunderously. Naturally we quietened our conversations and huddled in an attempt to comfort each other. But despite our best efforts we were overcome and all of us cried, feeling helpless. Still crying, I called my sister. All I said was, "Can you come home? They're fighting again." And no sooner had I hung up the phone then she had burst through the front door, bravely fighting tears and ready to shut down the argument. The Rose.

I am not kidding when I say it was rough terrain. Living in a house where the tension is so high you do not even want to invite your friends over is not fun. When you have one parent who is preparing to separate and the other who is passively avoiding help or unwilling to change to make the marriage healthy again. I remember when we had been supporting Mum and Dad for months and it had reached a point where we sat them down and respectfully gave them an ultimatum. This was the last straw. They needed to get professional help for their marriage or else The Rose and I were going to take our younger siblings and move out. At twenty and nineteen, we had been prepared to do whatever it took to keep our family together, even if it meant leveraging our young ones. We figured out that between her full time and my part time wages we could afford a decent three-bedroom place, enough food and to keep her car on the road, as well as to pay for the kids' schooling. We were prepared to fall behind on our personal saving goals for the sake of saving our family. And it was the wake-up call my parents needed to get their acts together and well, we live to tell the tale.

THE UNGLAMOROUS

Diary, I learned some hard truths. Pain in this life is inevitable; how I navigate that pain, and subsequent healing process, determines the resilience with which I can face life's bigger, more brutal battles. I know that does not sound too glamorous, and the truth is it definitely is not. I sometimes wish I could ease the blow or absorb the shock or even sugar-coat it, but I think I would much rather the momentary discomfort of truth than the agonising pain of deception.

Our family just kind of takes hit after hit after hit. Eventually there is that one dog shot that knocks the wind right out of you and all of a sudden Tyson is out. We were fighting for our family to stick together and, like a champion, my warrior of a sister was leading from the front.

Is it a surprise that the effects of my parents' struggling marriage showed in the form of my brother running away from home, getting into brawls and pursuing a toxic relationship of his own? Is it a coincidence that at this time he was conveniently at a crossroads in his life where he had more than enough reasons to call it quits on his faith and take advantage of the drugs that were so easily accessible to him? We would be naïve to think he did not entertain the pull to roll with the gangs of Western Sydney as he chose to rub shoulders with the 'crowd going nowhere'. He too fell into the trap of seeking answers at the bottom of a bottle. Thank God it was a vain pursuit!

For my younger sister, her struggle manifested in a destructive eating disorder. When she felt helpless and that the fate of our parents' marriage was out of her control, the one thing she could control was the food nourishing her body. And when you are feeling devalued you do not particularly place value on your body. Dog shot.

As for me? Well I developed some very ugly thorns around my heart and wore my daddy issues loud and proud. I made sure it was obvious that I could not stand him. I made sure he felt like he was not worthy of my eye contact, let alone my conversation. I made sure it was obvious he knew he had screwed up. I wanted nothing more than to make him feel like he could never have any close relationship with me again. And because Hawaii was a disaster trip of tension and awkward vibes, I blamed him. Everything that was not enjoyable about our family now was instantly his fault. Our entire dynamic changed. We were divided and it was all because of him. In my heart I held onto bitterness like a lifeline and I encouraged my mum to leave him. I know the more honourable thing to do would have been to fight for our family to stay together and for my parents to work through their problems. But if I am being completely transparent, I wanted them to separate and eventually divorce. I wanted it because then at least I could blame my dad for all the hurt and pain I was harbouring inside. At least all the rebellious things I wanted to do could be validated by a broken home. And since I could not control my intense sense of rejection, I was going to be an ice queen of a daughter and never make it easy for him to even have a conversation with me. I wanted him to feel left out of my life. I wanted him to beg to be accepted again. I wanted to control our relationship now. And I wanted it to be clear that because he hurt me, I wanted nothing to do with him.

I was hurting, and too stubborn to admit that I really wanted nothing more than to have a restored relationship with my dad. I wanted him back. But I could not trust him. And I was nowhere near ready to forgive him. Honestly, I was in dire need of the affirmation and guidance only a father could give because at that point in my life I was so overwhelmed by my lack of self-worth that I was drawing it in a superficial sense from any male attention I was getting. I remember having a breakdown one day, feeling consumed with pressure to make a decision. There was one guy who was really good to me. And he was really serious about me. But I was stringing him along and I knew it. It was not fair. And I was also distracted by at least three other guys that were showing interest in me at the same time. On one hand it was fun and I liked being wanted. It stroked my ego. I played innocent bystander when I learned at least two of these guys were also already in relationships. In a twisted way, it made me feel good to be the girl that guys would want to break up with their girlfriends for. But on the other hand, I was freaking out because I did not know what to do or how to handle guys in their mid-twenties when I was only nineteen. I needed my dad to remind me of the girl he raised. I needed him to instil value and worth into me because I was feeling pressured to be with guys I did not want to be with. I thought I owed them my time and cheeky conversation because they paid me attention. At the same time I could also use this male attention to get back at my dad. I wanted him to see how much I was icing him out of my life and that I was going to make decisions like this without him. I remember saying out loud, "Just because he is my father does not give him the divine right to have a say about who I date or marry. That is a privilege and he does not have it anymore!" It was my cry for help. It hurt me to feel disconnected from my dad; and now I wanted to keep him at arm's length to minimise any more potential pain. Everything between us was going to be on my terms. But now it became clear he was not the only one that was hurting me. I was hurting me. But I was too proud to admit I needed him.

Everything was a struggle now. I was having breakdowns at work because I was scared my parents were going to split, and there was so much tension at home I did not want to be there. It was the fear of the unknown and I was in two minds about everything. *Do I want this to happen or don't I?* I remember reaching out to a friend and balling my eyes out saying I needed help because I was pretty sure I was losing my mind. I knew she had gone through some hard times recently and could recommend a good psychologist. And so began a painful period of healing.

BREATHE IN, BREATHE OUT

I realised I was gripping anger and bitterness with both hands and nothing about my stubborn hold was improving my relationship with my dad or my family dynamic. I had to make a decision. Did I really want my dad to be a distant father for the remainder of my life? Or did I actually have it in me to forgive him and change my behaviour to reflect that forgiveness? I made him work hard for my eye contact. I made him work hard for my conversation. But if I had decided to forgive him then my actions had to line up with that. Despite how I felt about it and how much I knew it would hurt to swallow my pride, I could not escape the longing I had for a healthy relationship with my dad. I also could not ignore how exhausted I felt staying angry all the time. It was the most draining attitude I had ever had. It sapped the energy out of me. But the moment I decided I was done with being angry, the release gave me a peace like I have never felt before. I felt like I could breathe properly for the first time in a while. Holding onto my anger felt like I was squeezing and pulling a rope with all my might. And because I was putting all my energy into tightening my grip on the rope, I did not realise I was holding my breath as well. But letting go … wow! It let the blood circulate around my body and the oxygen fill my lungs again. It let the heat drain from my head and it reminded my heart that it had capacity to love even after being hurt.

I must admit it was not easy. I must admit there were some days I wish I had not decided to be a better person because it was tempting to revert back to being angry again when things seemed a little hard. It was hard to watch my mum cry and heal and cry and heal some more. It was hard to support marriage counselling because pride has a way of keeping your pain silent until it has eaten away at every good thing inside you. Once I was able to accept that no family is perfect and no marriage is perfect, I got past the embarrassment of Mum and Dad getting help. Some days I wished I never woke up early to hear the argument or chase after my mum as she left the house crying. Some days I wished we could be a fake family for once and sweep all our problems under a rug. But that was not my reality. I did not realise how much the healing journey of my parents' marriage would profoundly impact me. It forced me to consider the importance of who I chose to marry. Watching my parents stick it out through a painful season made it obvious to me that it takes a strong and determined couple to persevere through situations many would have called it a day on. I admire them and their conviction to keep their vows and honour each other before God through hurt and hoorays.

Maybe bravery can be premeditated. Maybe as we keep going through life, different circumstances force us to use different measures of *brave* from our internal store space. What do you think Diary?

BRAVERY: FROM PREMEDITATED TO SPONTANEOUS

Around two years later I was in Melbourne on a girl's trip with a friend. We roamed the grid like locals and shopped like housewives. We drank good coffee and took post-worthy selfies in the trendiest spots the city had to offer. We were young, independent women and we were out and about, just living our best lives. At that particular point in my life I had a fun job that I genuinely enjoyed, I was making head way on personal goals and was the proud owner of my first car. I was undeniably in love with my best friend of two years and he was in love with me. We entertained plans for our future and were irrevocably infatuated with each other. Oh and … I was also on the mend from a deteriorating mental health state; a dark secret I kept close to my heart.

What a vibe killer.

Has it ever bothered you to hear someone comment on how strong you are? I do not mean physical strength (but well done if you are smashing PR's on your bench press, brother. I am proud of you). I mean your resilience. When you are going through hell and people attempt to encourage you by saying 'wow, you're so strong', or 'I don't know how you are doing it, but I just admire your strength', or my personal favourite 'I know it's hard, but God gives His hardest battles to His strongest warriors'. Excuse me for a moment whilst I bury my head in a cushion and scream with all my might. Politely nodding when people make comments like that is about all I can manage. For me, these are not compliments. They do not encourage me, not even in the slightest. Can I be brutally honest with you? (I am going to have a bratty moment here.) I might lose all self-control and punch the next person who says I am strong. It is easy to make these comments when you get your weekly, bi-monthly or annual update on my life, because you are not in the blood bath of a battle it is to live through it every day. OK, end rant. My moral of the story is RESILIENCE is hard. (Would it kill ya to lend me a shoulder to cry on?)

I had to learn some hard things about grief. I had to learn some intense things about trauma. I had to reteach myself how to deal with pain, fear and stress. I had just turned twenty-one and although this was a profoundly momentous milestone for me, it also brought to the surface a lot of grief I had buried from the traumatic pain of losing my big sister, The Rose, earlier that year …

BRAVE OR BURNT OUT?

You see, twenty-year-old Brooke was quite possibly the busiest person on Earth. And she knew it. And she owned it. I was a hard worker and gaining lots of momentum in my role, successfully building a client base and never saying no. I was faithfully serving as a junior high school youth leader in my church's youth ministry, mentoring young girls in their spiritual growth. I was meticulously planning my 21st birthday and saving every penny to have a banger of a party. I was hardly ever home and operated on three to five hours of sleep every night. I would schedule catchups with friends three weeks in advance to fill my one free night a week. I became the world's most efficient multitasker and micromanaged my days by the hour. My pace was fast, and I did everything to keep it that way because I knew that if life slowed down there would be just enough quiet for me to be stuck with my thoughts and my reality. And they were much too painful to deal with.

I reached breaking point when, amid my busy schedule, I had made regular timeslots to meet with a counsellor who had advised me to strip my life back and focus on my mental health. I learned that there is a scary stage of grief that sees your body kick into 'auto-pilot' whilst your mind goes AWOL. From the outside you appear to be still doing life as normal, but internally you are unaware. I would frequently have episodes where I 'blacked out', you could say. I would suddenly click back into reality and have no recollection of the previous hour or two of my life. Sometimes I would find myself 'come to' sitting in my car at work without any idea how I even got there. I could not remember waking up in the morning or dressing myself and I definitely could not remember driving, but now I was sitting here. I wish I could say it had only happened a handful of times and it was easy to shake off. But it did not and it was not and I had full blown panic attacks every time.

I came to learn that you can be in a complete state of numbness and have little to no grip on your mind. It scared the life out of me and it forced me to come face to face with some raw heartaches that desperately needed my attention. It was a most gruelling six-month journey of recovery.

So, Diary, here is what happened. There is exactly nineteen and a half months that separate me and The Rose. She looks like our dad and acts like our mum. I look like our mum and act like our dad. She has straight hair and I have curly hair. We were always together and she was always one of the most influential people in my life. Losing her is agonising; I had not known a pain like this even existed. I do not think it would be fair to allow you to believe that she died. When I say 'lost', I mean she left. She just went missing one day and as of today it is just shy of four years since she decided not to return home.

You should know that nobody has challenged me in my pursuit for *Robust Love* more than my sister. Although she has not been in my life for the past few years, even from a distance she is teaching me how to love unconditionally. She is teaching me how to differentiate authentic love from the deception of 'true love'. She is teaching me how vital it is to have a deep revelation of my God as Love. I know this because she has been baited and entrapped by a toxic kind of love. She has been fooled by the cheapest version of it. It is the kind that sniggers and conspires to drive wedges between her and her family. It is the kind that emotionally manipulates and prepares appetising banquets of lies to cloud her judgement. It is the kind that promised freedom only to imprison her in its jealous grasp. It is the kind that saw the delicate beauty of The Rose and snatched her when she was vulnerable.

Why did it hurt so much when my older sister left? I had known nothing but her love and protection my entire life and as we grew up I never doubted her loyalty to our family; her honour and respect for our parents; her firm convictions in her faith; and her motherly nature towards caring for me and my younger siblings. Her generous spirit and joyous nature were ingrained in every fibre of her being and her open heart – liberally loving and welcoming people into her care was foundational to her character. She patiently nurtured and led humbly. The way she carried herself was gracious and admirable. So what could be more heartbreaking than seeing all of that being extinguished by the toxicity of one person?

No one opened their arms wider than my sister. She was generous in every sense of the word – with her time, money, encouragement, friendship. The journey we have been on with her over the past three and a half years has proved that this beautiful quality has also become a fatal flaw. When your heart is so big for people, sometimes you are blinded to their underlying motives. Because she always wanted to see the best in people, she neglected the wisdom to always consider the consistency of fruit in their lives. And this was the devastating case when one friend in particular schemed their way into my sister's life, infiltrating influence into every area and determined to leave no stone unturned. My sister has never been an easily pressured person. Like the story of many who have grown up subject to bullying, she had her fair share of years lacking in confidence with a depleted self-esteem, but she overcame and discovered her identity; walking confidently through life. She knew how to say no to things and people who threatened to challenge her core values. But if you give a manipulative, self-seeking and toxic person the right circumstances they will snatch the opportunity to take advantage of a moment of vulnerability without hesitation. And that is how my sister's achilles heel was clipped. She was vulnerable. And then she was snatched.

This friend, whom we will call TJ, came into our lives like all of our friends have. Each friend is included in our family; you are never just the friend of one, you are a friend of all. We are a package deal. So it was not uncommon that within a short time of TJ being introduced to us we quite often had this new friend of ours over at our house for meals and movies, attending sporting events and birthday celebrations as we all built relationship. One thing that has always been said of our family, and we consider one of the greatest compliments, is how well we love others and how naturally inclusive we are. It was no different with this new friend. Our home was always open and we genuinely enjoyed TJ's company. Our hilarious times together were because we shared a lot of things in common, like a passion for sport, a love for food and family and maximising quality time. It was clear TJ was becoming one of the most frequent visitors to our home and cementing a close friendship with my sister, which we were happy to support. Over time however, certain actions started to cause friction in our family. TJ was comfortable around us, but this began erring on the border of disrespect when my sister started being influenced to rebel against my parents and to distance herself from our family.

The Rose's moment of vulnerability came after an exhausting bout of rejection from some extended family members around one of the most momentous occasions in her life: her 21st birthday. She was back-stabbed and gossiped about. She was disrespected and ignored. She was made to feel unimportant and altogether devalued. And this all came from people she loved the most. The people she went out of her way for, time and time again. The people she generously gave of herself to. She did her best to be brave and shake it off, extending grace and kindness like only she can with a heart so tender. But we all knew she was wounded deeply. And although her iconic smile redirected suspicions of sorrow, the light in her eyes faded a few shades dimmer and it was evident only to those who knew her best. I knew my sister's heart was sore. I hated seeing her that way. And I was determined to do everything I could to ensure her 21st birthday celebration was going to be as stress-free as possible because she deserved nothing but the best. We planned it meticulously for months on end; the centre pieces, the dress, the hashtags, the seating plan, the photo booth, the DJ. Everything was going to be just as she requested. Her 21st was something special, just like her. And our immediate family made a point of esteeming her and placing value on her. But she was discouraged with the lack of respect, love and decency owed to her from our cousins, not just because she was a human but because she was blood. And now she was desperate to feel loved and accepted.

The next twelve months was a heart-wrenching battle for her true identity. There was a rapid decline in everything that made up this exceptionally beautiful and astoundingly generous young woman until she became a shell of herself. She looked like my sister but she was not my sister. It was like watching a fresh apple rot over time. Every core value that made up her persona was choked and the lights completely went out in her eyes. She was hardly recognisable. And we fought hard for her. But so did this toxic friend, who fought savagely to be the most dominant voice in her life, and the dramatic changes we were seeing in my sister proved TJ had capitalised on her vulnerability and was succeeding at manipulating her to turn her back on the people who knew her the best and loved her the most.

We exhausted every resource we had to help my sister. We reached out to close friends and key mentors in her life to come alongside her. We had family interventions when we were noticing her weight drastically dropping until bones were protruding out from beneath once snug-fitting clothes. But during this time it seemed the only person she listened to was that new friend of hers. TJ had a hold over her that we could see was deliberately working against everything we as a family stood for and we tried to warn her multiple times how unhealthy this was for her. We went to family counselling together – we wanted to support her, and our family needed practical tips on how to move forward together despite the tension this friend was breeding in our home. TJ was overstepping boundaries; lying to my parents and challenging them on the way they parented; encouraging my sister to break curfew every week and to spend as little time at home as possible; interfering in private family matters and asserting self-appointed authority over my younger siblings. TJ was a constant voice in my sister's ear and she was becoming less and less the open-hearted, loving and generous sister I knew her to be. She was becoming easily angered, uninterested in our family, argumentative and rebellious.

I remember after one of our family counselling sessions we drove to a park. We were exhausted from going around in circles with the psychologist and emotionally drained. My sister sat at the bench uninclined to acknowledge the profound concern the rest of us had for her. It was obvious TJ was driving a wedge between us but she was not bothered with giving any of us eye contact. She gripped her phone, which over the course of some months had now become glued to her person like an additional limb. Dressed like a boy, a style change we knew was far from her usual presentation and heavily influenced by her friend, she showed no emotion. She was cold. We asked if she could see the divide in our family and that the common denominator in these scenarios was TJ. She agreed. Then we asked if for the sake of our family's health she would drop this toxic friendship. She said *no* …

She said no. She said no? That's right. She said no.

Instantly we knew she had switched her loyalty from our family to TJ and it grieved us heavily. You know, Diary, it is painful to watch someone you love make choices that do not just hurt them but hurt you too. It is even worse when you know they are not in a position to make the wiser choices for themselves, but you cannot make those choices for them. The Rose was in close proximity to us, but emotionally and mentally so far removed. We kept extending our hands and love, but she was too busy. Her head was being filled with lies about our family and my parents. She was enticed with the promised gain of the world and an unrestrained freedom. She was baited with stunts of rebellion, little-by-little until TJ had her full allegiance. And then she was hooked with the closer: love to fill the void of value she missed when she was vulnerable.

Snatched.

It was the night before my little sister's 18th birthday party and we were busily preparing decorations and paper bag lanterns to line the driveway. It was late and we were tired but a confession came that widened all our eyes. The Rose admitted to being in a secret romantic relationship with this toxic friend we were all struggling with. She was upset and admitted she knew it was wrong and that it needed to end. We could not have agreed more. We wanted her back; the real her. She was our blood and we hated seeing her manipulated and moulded into something she was not. She called to end the relationship on the spot. Our family sat at the kitchen table semi-shocked but mostly processing. We were not supposed to keep secrets like that from each other. We were not supposed to choose others over our own flesh and blood. We were not supposed to let anything or anyone come between us … And then there was knocking at the front door.

We fell silent.

It was after eleven o'clock at night but we all knew who it was. My sister's ex of ten minutes was outside. What started as knocking got more aggressive. It became beating. We could hear TJ yelling my sister's name and demanding us to open up and let her out. We heard screaming and insults being hurled at our family, accusing us of keeping her prisoner and calling my parents unfair names. We barricaded the door as TJ managed to force open our locked screen door and was now kicking down our front door. My dad and brother were pushing to keep the door shut and in the corner of the room my younger sister trembled with fear. Everyone was yelling. It was like a scene from a movie. I could hear my heart thudding loud and hard. I could not believe she was trying to force her way into our home. I could not believe she was scaring my family and provoking my dad and brother to fight.

I'll never forget the drama of that night. We experienced first-hand how psychotic and possessive this person was over my sister. What is more, I witnessed in person an immediate shift in my sister the moment she heard TJ's voice. It was like she snapped into a completely different person. When she had just confessed and unloaded her heavy secret on my parents, it was the first time we had seen the real her in months. It was her. But the moment the voice got in her head she snapped into a robot. She was like a dog obeying its master. It became real to us that my sister was being dominated and it was ugly. The police came to remove TJ from our property and to take statements as well as assess damage, warning her not to return again. But she was not going to let my sister go. And not only did TJ forever tarnish the memory of my little sister's 18th birthday party, she had the nerve to show up to our home a few days later in spite of the warnings received, forcing us to contact the police again.

I had never seen my big sister so weak before. She spent days in bed unable to speak or eat. She was like a baby. The intensity of such traumatic events like these and the constant emotional tug-of-war she found herself in had her drained of energy. She cried constantly and we fed her spoonfuls of oats just to get something in her system. She developed a curious shake in her hand that we sought medical attention for. One could say her body could not handle the trauma of the recent episodes. She was not medically fit to work or drive. For two weeks we took care of her whilst keeping a watchful eye on the driveway in case our door was about to be kicked open again. We knew TJ would stop at nothing to own my sister. She was mentally and emotionally manipulative and in no way, shape or form a healthy relationship in her life, or our family's lives for that matter.

And then, about two weeks later, three days shy of The Rose's 22nd birthday, she was able to return to work and had been dropped to work that morning by my mum. That afternoon I came home with my brother and we were met by two constables at the front door. They had been sent to our home to settle a domestic dispute between my sister and my parents. The only thing was my parents were not home and my sister was at work. My brother and I proceeded to explain the events that happened that night a few weeks earlier and then, mid conversation with now confused policemen, my mum pulled up. She had just gone to my sister's work to pick her up and was told she left at lunchtime and never returned to work. So here we were, my mum, brother and I with two officers trying to make sense of everything. Technically no one had confirmation on my sister's whereabouts, so was she now a missing person? We had a fairly confident idea who she was with, though.

That is the day my sister went missing. That is the day she left us. That is the day she walked away from our family and never came home. She changed her number and took all of her savings out of her account. She returned a few weeks later with a police officer and a notice of demand to collect all her belongings and moved in with her partner. Yes, she went back to that person. No, it has not been made easy for her to see or talk to us. Yes, she has been convinced to believe that we pushed her away. Yes, she has been made into a little puppet. She has cut our family off. We are blocked on all forms of social media. We siblings do not even know what we did wrong.

And no, we have not stopped fighting for her and loving her. Diary, I wonder if things would have panned out differently if The Rose's partner was a male.

I wonder how aware her circle of friends would have been of how emotionally manipulative, toxic and abusive this relationship was if they were not being so conscious of being politically correct.

I wonder if we, as her family, would still have been painted as religious and discriminative, rather than protective and concerned for her well-being if TJ was a boy.

Diary, resilience is hard.

It has ripped me raw to learn how to do life without her. She has missed many a milestone in the last three and a half years of mine and my younger sibling's lives. She has missed many birthdays – but not for a lack of invitations. She has missed holidays and family trips – but, again, not for a lack of inclusion. She has missed house moves and job promotions and every big moment in my brother's accelerating sporting career. She has missed Christmases and New Year's celebrations. She has missed the cakes we have bought on her birthdays to honour her even though she is not with us.

I miss her terribly. The day she decided to leave us I was left with her role to fill. But I was the support sibling; I did not know how to be 'the oldest'. I was not anything like her; I am still not anything like her. She will never be someone who is easily forgotten or replaced. But I had to step up. I always had my older sister to look to and depend on. But now I am the older sister; the only present older sister; the only active older sister. And on top of dealing with my grief of her absence in secret, I was desperately trying to put up a strong front so that my younger siblings felt safe and secure. I wanted them to feel like if they were not strong enough to cope, it was OK because I would be strong for them. Only I was dying on the inside. I felt like I was wearing shoes five sizes too big for me and it was obvious I could not pull it off. I often broke down in my car, feeling like a failure of an older sister because I could not be her. And I could not even be me without her. That is how much she impacted my life. That is how close we were. Siblings share an unspeakable bond. It is unique. It is a sibling soul tie. We were the fantastic four: The Robertson Kids. *How do we be us without her?*

We have all been impacted differently by her absence

from our lives. For my baby sister, depression suffocated her and she was robbed of her zeal for life. Her heart was broken, and she was grieving the loss of her big sister. Depression hung thick over her and she became trapped under this dense cloud for at least nine months. She moved out of our room and in to The Rose's room just to feel closer to her.

And then here I was with a frequently absent mind. A pain burrowed so deep I almost convinced myself it did not hurt anymore. I had become a shell, robotic in my routine. In the moments I was present-minded and alone, I found myself entertaining destructive thought patterns: I could justify running red lights. I often sized up telegraph poles to determine the severity of potential injuries if I decided to ram them. I was tired; exhausted by the fight of life. I wanted to call it quits. I envied patients in ICU and thought if I could crash my car and end up there with them, at least I would not have to do life for a few days while I recovered. And if I died? Well, that meant I was not living in pain anymore.

I had to allow myself to acknowledge and process feelings of hurt and betrayal. I had to deal with feeling abandoned. I had to seriously work on my heart and its default setting to snatch back its loyalty. I had to keep remembering Mum's wise words about forgiveness and to practice it. Again. And again. I had to deal with the intense waves of emotion that would hit out of nowhere, just missing her. Even in a practical sense, adjusting my default response to everyday situations; it is weird to ask for a table of five rather than six when that has been your only response your whole life. It is awkward to tip toe around innocent questions like, "Oh, where's your sister?" or "How's your sister going, we haven't seen her in a while?" or "How's your family doing?" I sorely miss her. Resilience is hard.

I recently sat in court and listened to absurd allegations made against my dad on behalf of my sister. I have never seen her look so unhealthy. Her weight is at the opposite end of the spectrum now, she is the biggest she has ever been. It looks like she is struggling to walk. She smells of cigarettes and looks unkempt. She is ice cold. There is no emotion in her face, like that day at the park. She is monotonal and well-coached in false accusations. I cannot explain how ridiculous it felt to be sitting there listening to the magistrate read my sister's statement of the night her partner bashed on our door. Somehow the facts of that night have turned into my dad becoming physically violent and pinning my sister against the wall by her throat. *Is this real life? Is there really an AVO being put against my father for something he never did? Is my sister really betraying her family like this? Is she really that brainwashed that she would rather be dishonest on a legally submitted document than to admit she is in dire need of rescuing from an abusive relationship that is forcing her to sever all ties to her family? Is society that concerned about 'equality' that it is willing to turn a blind eye to common sense and sound judgement of character when an entire family hangs in the balance?* Resilience is not just hard, Diary, it feels impossible.

I feel like I have been missing a part of me, a part of my body. We are not our family without her. We are officially one short. The worst part is she is not even deceased. She is alive and living within driving distance from us. She still works on the same street as my mum. She still attends the same church we attend. She just chooses not to have anything to do with us and it has felt like no matter who we have reached out to, to help us reconcile our family, the common cop-out response is 'she's an adult'. But she's my sister first and I love her very much. And if she ever finds this book in her hands, I want to make it clear that I will never give up on her. She is lost and well worth the pain of fighting for. She is well worth the oceans of tears I have cried and the countless rejections I have copped any time I have attempted to reach out. She is worth the heartache.

I want to admit to you, Diary, that this entry was very raw for me to write. I have stopped numerous times to cry. For the most part, learning to be *brave* without The Rose's example to follow means I have had to dig deeper than ever. Sometimes I am not sure I have any brave left in me. And sometimes it comes in spontaneous bursts. Maybe that is the beauty of bravery. Maybe, like roses, bravery has a strong side and a vulnerable side.

I could give you a dozen stories and reasons to be brave, just like I could give you a dozen roses. But here is the one parting truth I leave with you: *there is beauty for ashes.*

Consider this my single stem rose to you.

Love,

B xx

Ps. Dear Rose, #theresaspaceforyou.

IV

CLEAN VESSEL

Is BRAVERY just for me or is it for others?

I have a deep-spirited friend. Her name is Sarah. And I am convinced that when we were spirit beings in heaven, before being assigned to our families on Earth, we were inseparable. Our souls are connected. Our friendship is a place Holy Spirit gladly takes up residence. Sarah has a tenderness of heart I am yet to come across in another human. Encouragement is her native tongue and if there was anyone in this world I would want to be more like, it would be her. She has a reverent sensitivity to the prompting of Holy Spirit and the enveloping love that oozes from her heart knows no bounds. She has a prophetic gift and is well in tune. Her loyalty is undying. Her faith is unwavering. Her words hold weight in my life. She is my soul sister.

I sat across from her on the balcony of a corner café and poured my heart out about the evil that was ripping my family apart. She sat with me for six hours. I ranted and cried and ranted and cried some more. I shot rhetorical questions at her and then sulked, in denial that I knew the answers already. Transparently I confessed my default mentalities, and then corrected myself with the resolves I knew I needed to have if I was ever going to develop perseverance enough to see this hardship through to the end. I needed her to encourage me. I needed her to deliver a strong pre-battle pep talk. I needed her to give me something to cling to because I was on the frontlines of a waging war for the restoration of my family. I needed hope and reassurance that I, that we, would make it out.

Sarah does this thing where she sits and listens – like really listens. She is patient in every sense of the word. She does not break eye contact either (which for me is a super uncomfortable experience if I have just met you, but luckily you and I are friends, and Sarah and I are friends, so we are good). She nods occasionally and leans in attentively. I can't explain how I know this, but I just do … Without fail, every single time I find myself in these deep conversations with my soul sister I guarantee you she speaks on behalf of Holy Spirit. I have a theory that whilst she is 100% engaged in our physical conversation, her spiritual ears are listening intently to the voice of God, so that when it comes to her turn to respond she gives sweet vocal expression to His counsel. I know this to be true because I can see His Spirit is comfortably at home in her.

Sitting there in that café I was desperate to know that she was with me, and that if I was going to carry the full weight of this war season she would be right alongside me in the battle. I needed to know that if I was taking hit after hit after hit in the ring that she was in my corner; round one or round twelve. I needed to know that when I was feeling weak and crushed that she was contending for me on her knees. I needed to know that even if no one else was going to stick it out with me that she was going to be there no matter what.

Sarah spoke into me iron resolve that day. She lifted my gaze and she reminded me of the goodness of my God. Having reassured me that she was in the fight with me always, she spoke profound words that have foreshadowed every decision I have made from that day forward. She said, "B, Holy Spirit wants you to know that you're a clean vessel. Not a perfect one but a clean one. One who has cleared passageway for Him to work through, especially in this season with your family. He can trust you."

DETAILS AND DESIRES

I do not know what it is about purchasing your first car, but if you do not name it you are not living life to the fullest. It is true. Everyone knows there is an unspoken code that first cars must be named or else they are not worth driving (and you lose street cred). You have got to give it a cool name too; something that can be easily shortened and reflective of your car's personality. Another unspoken rule is that you get extra points if the name creatively rhymes or is alliterated. My first car was a steal and I was over the moon excited to be his proud new owner. (By the way, is third hand ownership a thing? I am asking for a friend!) For lack of a better word, he was a bomb. But he was my bomb and I affectionately named him Harvey (after Harvey Spector from the TV show *Suits* … If you have not watched this show, I am terminating our friendship effective immediately and will pray for God's mercy on your poor soul). He was 'Harvey the Hyundai' or 'The Harv' for short. (We were obviously on a nickname basis.)

Why did I choose this name, I hear you ask? Well, if you have watched the show, you would know right off the cuff that you are either Team Harvey or Team Mike. I do not think there is confusion about where my loyalty lies. Harvey Spectre is a well-respected, big shot lawyer. And in case you were wondering, he is a total stud. He is arrogantly intelligent but low-key thoughtful. He is hard to impress and flirts with law-abiding boundaries. One thing you will learn about Harvey is that he never misses a beat. Ever. Even when you are panicking that he is about to be blindsided by the backstabbing scandals of the Pearson Hardman law firm, he surprises you with the greatest, most intelligent (sometimes very cheeky) recoveries. He is a confident one-man show and his intelligence proves reliable in the most nail-biting close calls. Nothing seems to catch him by surprise. He does not always let on, but he knows all the details.

My Harvey and I have been through some interesting

times. He is a trooper. Can I tell you something ironic? God has a sense of humour because Harvey was an answer to prayer for me – literally. And I had no idea that he would also be the thing that caused me to pray even when I did not feel like it. He would be the thing that forced me to be vulnerable in my worship. He would be the safe place I retreated to and where I cried tears of anguish or wrote letters of healing. He became my portable war-room. Ask Sarah. She will tell you that every single time we rode in Harvey, God spoke, we cried and prayed and worshipped and His presence was with us.

Harvey was my personal *heart check* meter. I am serious. I told people all the time that 'God speaks to me through my car'. Here is the deal, if I had a heart issue I had not addressed, Harvey would not start. Now I know you are probably thinking that it is a coincidence or that Harvey was old so he most likely struggled to start at the best of times. And whilst you make a valid point, I am telling you the honest truth. I promise you, whenever he did not start I simply stopped and prayed about that issue I was avoiding, then next thing I knew we were away. It is pretty cool to think that God would care enough about my heart to be that practical.

There were times I was angry about something and left the house with attitude. But I did not get very far because Harvey would not start until I took a deep breath and prayed a very sincere, "Here you go Jesus, you can have this heart issue." And there were definitely times I thought I could get away with seemingly minor things; key word, *'seemingly'.* I remember a particular morning hopping in the car and still feeling offended by a friend I had seen the night before. I turned the key and Harvey did not start. I tried again. Still no luck. I was so sure I did not have a heart issue to address so I tried for a third time and he still would not budge. I knew exactly what it was by that point and I smacked the wheel, rolled my eyes and whinged, "Fine, God! There! I give you my bitterness." I was not impressed at all, because I honestly felt like I was justified and my friend was way out of line for what she had said to me. But sometimes you have to choose between holding a grudge and having a working car. I chose the working car.

I also remember a very expensive period of time with Harvey. Yeah, 'ol' mate' started costing me an arm and a leg. It felt like every week something was going wrong and urgently needed to be fixed. So I helplessly watched money drain from my accounts; flat tyres and a flat battery, a new fuel pump, new filters, high tension leads and new ignition chips – gosh the list went on and on. Honestly I could have bought a new car by the end of it. I had been working harder than hard and saving for a trip to Canada. It was my travel goal for that year and I was determined to reach it. But man! It felt like the goal posts kept getting pushed further and further away as I was now pouring more money into keeping Harv on the road than I was putting into my savings. Remember when I said that God spoke to me through my car? Well He also speaks to me through Sarah when I do not pay attention to Him. And this message was a hit up and a half …

MONEY, CARS & CONVICTION

I sat across from Sarah again, this time in one of Granville's best charcoal chicken spots. She was doing the sitting and listening thing again. And I was talking. Again. (I realise it sounds like I am not much of a good friend to Sarah – I promise I am, I even let her hug me! That is an inside joke. Never mind.) This time I was explicitly filling her in on some of my least honourable moments. I was in the thick of compromise – making decisions with no wisdom. Decisions that were dishonouring my parents and the guy I loved. And, worst of all, God. I frequently shoved morals and standards into the backseat as I took over control of the wheel and, without integrity, drove full speed down a road laden with 'Stop' and 'Danger Ahead' signs. I had let my guard down so much and started making small compromises that soon snowballed until I was knee-deep in mud. I was stuck. Knowing that what I was doing was wrong, I could not stop. I was not able to say *no*. And honestly, I did not want to say *no* because doing things in the dark and living dangerously close to the edge was fun and exciting and it felt real good.

I complained about how much money Harvey was costing. I vented my frustration and disappointment that my trip to Canada was moved for the third time in less than six months. She and I worked out that all the money I had spent so far to fix Harvey would have paid for my trip – more than once. Ouch! I only trusted a select few with the details of that few months of having no boundaries. (Or in my case, setting the boundaries and then removing them whenever it was convenient.) I had become a walking contradiction; full of deceit and a slave to my selfish desires. I was not the girl I said I was. And this girl was heading straight into a pit of destruction – the worst part was, I was willing. I remember struggling to look Sarah in the face as I confessed some of the things I had been up to by cover of night over that past fortnight. She lovingly let me attempt to justify my actions, but I already knew that I was not fooling her. She looked back at me and said, "B, you know I love you. And you know I am always going to back you. But if you keep these things up, two core values of yours are in jeopardy. They are your intimacy with God and your relationship with your family."

I tried to play it cool with a half-smile but inside I froze. Damn. She was spot on. It hit me like a tonne of bricks. Everything I was getting up to behind everyone's back was causing me to drift further and further away from close proximity with my God. The God my parents raised me to believe in and honour. The God I went to church to worship every week. That God, who was foundational to my person, suddenly had become less significant in view of all the things I selfishly wanted to pursue to make me feel good. And this was causing friction between me and my family. Sarah continued, "And sis, if this is what it is costing you financially, just imagine what it is costing you spiritually."

Flip. It was a double whammy. Game over. She was bang on again and I was dumb-founded. This whole time I was arrogantly thinking I could get away with doing things I should not have been doing, and completely oblivious to God trying to send clear warnings that these decisions were going to cost me more than just my savings for Canada and my integrity. These unwise decisions were very expensive ones, and I paid with my heart. Sarah gave me a steak to chew on and I was struggling to swallow it. *How did I let myself get to this point? How do I fix it? And how do I make the right decisions now with the least amount of pain?*

After that night I felt a deep, deep unease about where I was and who I had become. I felt sick in my stomach because I knew that the only way to fix things was to lay down something that I was not willing to let go of just yet. I am going to have a very vulnerable moment with you right now: I am not proud of the things I compromised on. Even more so, I am devastated at how cocky I was to ignore the warnings every time I was about to do something I never should have done. I was dabbling in lust-driven intimacy and I felt justified because I wanted desperately to have something in my life that made me feel good. I was hanging onto it because it represented security for me. When everything was a fight in my life, this was the thing that I did not have to strive for. When my home was taken from me and my parents were taken from me. When my dreams to further study were taken from me and my sister was taken from me. Here was my knight-in-shining-armour with ocean eyes, vowing to love me. I was wanted. I was promised the world. I was being satisfied behind closed doors and I finally had something that was just for me.

It is amazing the things you will compromise on when you think you are going to marry someone. I do not just mean listening to your least favourite radio station or making yourself learn facts about their favourite sporting team. I mean the standards and values I had fought with all my might to protect for twenty-one years – those were the things I threw away in an instant for momentary satisfaction. This cost me more than I can even begin to explain.

And then I found myself struggling to breathe when the plans for our future together were ripped to shreds and our relationship came to an abrupt end. There I was, peeling the remains of my stomped-on heart off the ground. It was a messy road to recovery after that. I was nursing a wounded heart, hiding under a heavy blanket of shame and crawling my way back to wholeness. Diary, I will tell you all about that soon.

CUDDLE BEAR & ANSWERED PRAYER

I have a beautiful friend. We will call her Bear. I like this name for her because she is close to my heart the way a plush bear is to a young one. She is also the softest soul I know (but do not be misled, she is insanely brave too – possibly one of the bravest gals I know) and her friendship reminds me of the love and kindness of my God. She is warm and comforting like a cuddle and I love her a lot. Bear and I started doing life closely a few months after Jesus had held my trembling hand through some of the most painful wound-washing months of my heartbreak.

Have you ever cried out to God in the middle of your pain? *Whyyyyyyy?! Why God, why? Why am I enduring this? How is this good for me? Don't You see me here? Do You hear me? Are You with me when I am crying myself to sleep? Why is this happening to me?!* Those were my daily aching groans. But as the months of healing trekked on, these thoughts started to become less and less dominant and God started to show me a lot of hidden insecurities I had. He started to teach me a lot about my heart. He started to reveal to me a lot about His character and He was taking me to a depth of intimacy with Him that I had never been to before. I became painfully aware, as I squirmed through the sting of a regularly tended to wounded heart, that I was desperate to know there would be a bigger purpose in all of this. There had to be a reason I was ploughing a path in heavy snow, and soon enough my prayers started to change. I started having conversations with God about my heart. I inquired of Him about the way He intended to use my pain for good. And I found myself praying a simple, new prayer, "God, as much as I have been through the most heart-breaking healing journey that I never wish to endure again, I will gladly re-live the pain a hundred times over if you let this journey encourage even one person – just ONE – if it means I can show them the path that leads back to You."

I remember the night Bear texted me to say she could not breathe. Her relationship with her almost fiancé had just come to a shocking end and she was desperately gripping the hole in her chest where her heart had been violently ripped from. I cannot tell you how quickly my eyes filled with tears as my heart immediately identified with her pain. I felt helpless. I wanted so badly to have a time travel machine and to be able to fast forward us to the part where she is over her heartbreak and is happy again. I wanted so badly to protect her from the severe discomfort of raw wounds – the ones that are fleshy and exposed for everyone to see. A few days later I sat across from her in a booth at a café, prepared with a care pack and tissues; we were set, with our coffees ready to sip, to cry our way through her pain.

She began telling me the details of the events that lead to that devastating night and all I could do was give her my undivided attention and comfort her with the organic dark chocolate I knew she loved. I sat and listened. My heart hurt for her. As she was telling me elements of their relationship, it started to sound very familiar. She continued on, and then it started to sound almost identical. Our stories were twins separated at birth! Right down to the details of planning married life with our first loves and just waiting on the engagement ring. Oh wow. As I listened to her verbally process her hurt, I could not help but feel a sense of strength and hope because I knew her pain, but also because I knew a road to recovery. I knew the path that lead to healing. I knew the trail that lead to true love. I had a map and I could show her! We drank our hot beverages and cried together. We prayed together and formed a bond that to this day has withstood some very, very raw moments.

I remember driving home and praying – just talking with God, asking Him to help me be the friend she needed. I wanted guidance on how to lovingly let her heal at her own pace as well as tactfully spur her towards the harder things because I knew they would help her the most. In that moment I was reminded of the brutal healing journey I had been through myself and the nights of crying out *WHY.* And then I felt God finally answer me, "Bear is why." With those three words I felt an overwhelming sense of emotion and I cried the remainder of the drive home. I was not upset; it was more that I felt remembered. I know it sounds strange but I just felt so close to God. He remembered my weeping nights and He answered me so gracefully. At the time of my hurt He did not answer me right away, and yes I felt like He ignored my pain for a bit. But I can now acknowledge that He remained silent because my healing journey had to be for me, first. In order to heal the right way and as thoroughly as He allowed me to, I had to do it for me. I had to plough that snow on my own. Actually, it felt more like hopelessly shovelling a mountain of snow with a plastic spoon. But He heard me and He remembered me and He answered me. Then (let's just brag on how He is a God of details) He simultaneously gave me permission to lead the *one*. Do you remember? The *one* I had prayed to be able to help with my pain. And there it was. My heartbreak was not a waste of time. My healing was not in vain. My pain was validated.

THE OPERATING TABLE

'Healing' sounds smooth and balmy, doesn't it? Seriously, what a relaxing word? I do not know about you but when I think of 'healing' I automatically picture spa treatments and carefree vibes. (Insert record scratch here.) Well this is awkward, because healing is nothing like that. Sorry to interrupt your day dream. When Sarah spoke 'clean vessel' over me it had given me hope. It encouraged me to keep going even in the face of certain discomfort. I had no idea that the meantime would be so painful to navigate. I had no idea that my mental health was going to be attacked so savagely. I had no idea that I was going to endure heartbreak so devastating, that my entire frame was crippled from the impact. I had no idea there would be set backs to my goals and financial frustration. I had no idea I would have to muster all my bravery to give others hope. But what I had to cling to was that this God I had been fighting to keep faith in was going to use all of it. He was going to use me. He was going to work through me because I had made room for Him to work with. And He did just that.

SISTER'S KEEPERS & SHIELD HOLDERS

In my humbling months of healing and recovering from my mental health battle, one of the things I was advised to do was keep a journal. It was for the purpose of penning anything I wished. I could write as much or as little as I wanted to. The only rule was I HAD to write. I could record memories or leave notes for myself to remember how much I was progressing. The pages were ready and waiting. I had gleaned from wise counsel and I reluctantly decided the journal would be the best way for me to grieve and heal so I was going to write a journal for The Rose.

I stamped dates in every day that I wrote to her. I rotated specially bought pens with every new entry. And I wrote for months. I labelled the journal 'My Sister's Keeper' and filled it with letters and prayers for The Rose. I will not lie to you and say that writing in that journal was the easiest part of my day. I was often ripped raw and stained the pages with puddles of tears as I penned my pain. Some days I could not write in it. Some days I just grieved. I remember my trusted counsel saying that this journal was also going to be something that would help my sister heal from her brokenness when she eventually returns home. So, I fussed over the details with her in mind. But guess who else was present in the details? Yep, my God. Whilst I laboured in obedience to play a role in my sister's healing, here was God casually performing open heart surgery on me at the same time; sitting with me as I poured my heart onto the pages of that journal. He was healing me. He was refining me. He was restoring me. Just cleaning out all the gunk, one heartache at a time.

Diary, I think I am starting to get it now. I think I am starting to understand how fickle my heart is and how much I really do need to make the most of life's hardships and let them refine me. I think I am starting to see how every trait I admire in the brave people of my life will only be produced in me if I use my faith as a flaming torch in the dark tunnels of life's painful seasons. I think I am starting to see how bravery is required not just for me, but to give others permission to push on, despite their pain. I have been thinking that maybe when we are brave enough to be vulnerable, strength is built within us. Strength that is like a shield – broad enough for me and the people I find myself walking next to in life.

Thank You God for letting me keep friends like Sarah and Bear in my life! I really do not know where I would be without them. When I grow up, I want to be faithful enough to keep my heart as tender as Sarah's and brave enough to trust the healing process as gracefully as Bear.

Love,

B xx

V

WAX SEAL LOVE

Dear Diary,

Does BRAVERY promise a next chapter?

Psssst! Diary, I gotta tell ya, I am not excited about writing this entry. But I did promise to tell you all about it, and I keep my word. It has been raw; very raw to live through. And it has been excruciating to heal and extract a personal revelation from. I know you are probably thinking, *oh c'mon Brooke, you've been through a lot of things, and surely this isn't too bad*. As much as I really want to agree with you and just push myself to get over it and write, I just thought I would give you the heads up that I have been squirming and blankly staring with absolutely no idea where to start.

Maybe I will start with a confession … Yeah, let's do that. OK …

I had been working my little tail feather off to boost my savings and reach my goal of finally getting to Canada. (Yes! We got there in the end!) Initially, the purpose for going was to visit a beautiful friend who had recently moved back home after spending a couple of years studying in Sydney. But as I got closer and closer to my departure date, if I can be completely honest with you, Canada had become my way of running away. I was suffocating in the bubble of my life here in

Sydney and I desperately needed to get out. I could not take it anymore and was itching to escape the triangle of places I invested the majority of my time into, to get as far away as possible. I wanted out of Sydney. I wanted out of Australia. I wanted out of the whole stinking Southern Hemisphere. ASAP.

Canada represented a few firsts for me. My first solo trip overseas. My first time seeing snow. My first time celebrating my birthday in a different time zone. And it was my first breath of fresh air in a long, long time. I was finally oceans away from the problems that were sucking the life right out of me. Finally off the grid (yes, I travelled to the other side of the world with no phone or smart devices). And finally seeing wide open spaces and new landscapes to remind me that my God was bigger than the asphyxiating bubble I called my life. My incredible blessing of a friend, Kristen, who was waiting for me in Toronto, can vouch that I was coming out of a hot mess of an emotionally draining year. So I filled her in on all the details as we road-tripped to Niagara the moment I touched down in the promised land.

THE DREAM & THE DROP

So, my heart was broken. It was proper shattered. I wish there were words to describe the pain, but I do not think any I can manage to conjure up would do it justice. But I can attempt to describe a fitting visual for you. Imagine building a tall tower of dreams. Every level is like a future plan; built of your hopes and all the things you look forward to. The interior design on these levels is immaculate, every detail represents the depth of thought you have put into these hopes and dreams, and your future plans are pretty stylish (if you may say so yourself). The higher your tower gets the deeper your emotional investment becomes and the bolder you get with your level plans. You are proud of your tower; in fact, you try to casually slip it into conversations for a good old humble brag. You spend every day and night thinking about how to make your tower better. *Oh!* you think to yourself, *I will crown it with the most expensive glass ornament just for the top level,* the penthouse suite reserved for only your most elite dream. It is the most intimate of settings and the guest list maxes out at the 'plus one' of your choice – your forever one. So you give this priceless glass ornament to your chosen one as you both marvel at the view of the world from the balcony. There is nothing that can bring you down from this high; the view holds so much potential and it is simply beautiful, to say the least. You even start dreaming about the next tower to build together.

Then all of a sudden, the altitude makes it hard to breathe. Your chosen one starts to feel light-headed and woozy. He is not making eye contact with you anymore; he is just staring over the rail looking how far down it is to safety. And before you can ask him if he needs to sit down and breathe, his trembling hands fumble the priceless glass ornament and it freefalls in slow motion to meet the pavement waiting storeys and storeys below. Shattered.

You get the picture now don't you? (And hopefully my metaphorical heart scattered in pieces?) How do you even recover from that kind of drop? It was so high up; my tower was sculpted by my highest hopes and dreams, and now the lights were shut off and there I was, searching for the chards. *Seriously?* This is the point in the movie where I would lean over to you and say, "Flip. How much more could this poor poppet's heart take?" And well, actually that was my very real question to God, "What the heck?! As if I have not been through enough already!!! How much more can my heart take?" I found myself in the darkest pit. I was at my lowest point. And all I had now was a shattered heart and shame-stained rags. *How did I get here?*

HE LOVES ME ...

My best friend and I were as iconic and inseparable as B1 and B2 from that children's TV show, *Bananas in Pyjamas*. We knew each other's work, family and social schedules like the back of our hands, and even amongst all that busyness we managed to hang out at least four out of seven days a week. Sometimes it was a quickie Boost Juice after a boxing class or dinner at Sushi. At least once a week it was brunch at our go to café where he would order the big breakfast and I would order smashed avocado with poached eggs. I would trade the bacon off my plate for the sourdough on his and life was good. We made a point of checking out the latest kicks at Footlocker and passing the time people-watching with scoops of Ben and Jerry's. He was easily my favourite company to keep and we often joked about growing old in the same nursing home together just so we could keep the good times rolling until we kicked the bucket.

He was fiercely loyal. One time I drove my car into a brick pillar of a friend's garage door at the bottom of the steepest driveway known to mankind (I know right – how embarrassing!). Naturally I called him to come and tow my car and within ten minutes he was there. He left lunch with a mate and rushed over to help me. And when my car was back at the top and ready to be driven again, he followed behind my friend and me until we reached our destination, just in case anything happened to my car on the drive. What I did not know, but learned soon after we arrived, was he had food poisoning and when I called he had just thrown up his lunch. But he came to my rescue anyway. Yep, he was loyal.

When he was sick, I would drive over with his favourite orange juice and force him to drink it with a cap full of olive leaf extract. And when I was packing my days out and bouncing from one thing to the next, he would call to wake me up from my power naps to get ready to go again. He had sniffed a million soy candles with me until I found one I was crazy about and then surprised me with that candle and a handwritten note thanking me for being a good friend to him. When he had a bad day at work I left a parcel at his front door with his favourite snacks to boost his mood. Whenever either one of us were out and about (which was always) it was standard to keep the other in the loop with hilarious things we witnessed or experienced; things like amazing food we tried for the first time or shocking outfits we saw on strangers. On the rare occasions that we were out without each other, he wanted to know that I got home safely, and I wanted to know he got home safely. He was the last person I texted at night and I would usually wake up to a text or call from him in the morning since he started before the sun rose.

We were comfortable and familiar with each other. Not much happened in our lives that the other did not know about. We often laughed about how similar we were and on the regular occasion we would run into people we knew, we would skilfully dodge comments about unofficially being a couple. It seemed like on a weekly basis I was diffusing rumours or convincing people that he was not my boyfriend and I was not his girlfriend. It was the same for him too. We even started this segment in our catch-ups called 'story time' where we humorously retold awkward conversations we had had with someone else who pressured us to 'define the relationship'. We had a good thing going but we were in denial that we were developing the type of friendship that was confusing the heck out of our relationship status, and evidently everyone around us.

Well … I fell hard for my best friend. I loved him before we even admitted we had feelings for each other. My stubbornness and pride kept that secret from escaping my lips for a while. But my actions immediately gave me away like wearing fluorescent colours under a black light. He was everything I quietly desired in my heart; strong, knowledgeable, hard-working and funny. He reminded me a lot of my dad; a little rough around the edges and maybe, at first glance, easily misunderstood because life had given him a story worth telling too. But within seconds of interaction with him a soft heart surfaces and so how could that not make me feel safe?

And I knew I was quickly becoming the new benchmark for him. I was the opposite of his previous partner in every way. He was wounded badly and made a point of keeping an emotional distance from people to protect his heart from breaking again. But as we got closer he began lowering the walls and loosening his grip and allowing himself to feel again. And here we were with all this built up unspoken tension between us but neither one of us wanted to say anything for fear of losing our best friend.

I had never had a friend like him before. He made me so happy and frustrated at the same time. He was the smartest person I knew but also had some 'not so bright' moments. But I can't deny that he was simply the best person I knew. In some ways we could not be more opposite and in other ways we could not be more alike.

It was uncanny.

It was hilarious.

It was near perfect.

Needless to say that when that fateful day came when we sat in our regular booth at our go to café and I backed him into a metaphorical corner, teasing the truth out of him, we admitted our feelings and agreed that we would do everything we could to make this relationship go the distance. Neither one of us were willing to lose the other so we were determined to have mature conversations and reassess boundaries now that it was confirmed we meant more to one another than a funny meme and regular hangs. I knew that he was not looking for a superficial relationship; he was a handful of years older than me and looking to settle down. He knew I was not interested in playing the field and I had held out on being with someone for this long to be sure I would only date and marry one man. So why not do that with your best friend, right?

What a feeling! I felt like for the most part of our friendship I had been restraining an excitedly eager heart, and then the moment we committed to moving forward together it shot right out of my grip and raced across the table to glue itself to his. My best friend now thoroughly had my heart and it grew fonder and fonder of him with rapid momentum. Now our conversations were future-based, they were no longer *I-* or *me-*centred; they were *we-* and *us-*centred. I had never officially had a boyfriend before – yes, interest came and went over my teenage years, but nothing like him. I had entertained boys who noticed me, and when they flirted I flirted back for as long as it took until I got bored or there was another guy that was confident behind a screen. But he was the only one brave enough to talk to my parents and the respect he had for my family made him a thousand times more attractive to me. No one cared for me the way he did. He was always mindful of me and he said to me many times that he just wanted to make my life easy. He never wanted me to stress about anything, he wanted to fix everything and to make me smile and laugh. He wanted to be my husband and take care of me. Was this too good to be true? I wanted him with everything I had.

We soon had to reassess our boundaries because there was simply not enough accountability in our 'friendship routine' to keep us from getting away with things in our romantic relationship. From the beginning we decided together that we wanted to honour God with our relationship. We wanted it to be different from his previous ones and we wanted it to end with the goal of marriage. We wanted our families to be in support of us, and key people in our lives that we trusted to approve of it. So we got to work right away. I think one of the hardest changes we made was how often we hung out. We had to make sure we always had other people present too. See, our friendship was always casually just us and we were fine with it; but now we were putting every precaution in place to make sure we did not give into our raging hormones. That part was torture. I missed him because I saw him less, and then when I saw him I was fighting to keep burning desires at bay.

I was entirely infatuated with him. What little girl does not grow up collecting ideas and colours and songs for her dream wedding to her dream guy? He wanted to marry me, and I could not wait to give him every part of me. The conversations we had about our future were my favourite. The topic of us was my favourite. It was fun to dream together and talk about places we would go and the things we would do with our lives. He had a five-year plan and buying a house, moving overseas and pushing me to study were all top priorities. I saw a completely different side of him, a tender and vulnerable side that instantly made me weak at the knees for him. I loved watching his face as he passionately shared what he hoped for our future. I loved learning about his heart. I loved hearing him dream big dreams of the man he wanted to become and how much he honoured and respected my parents for the way they raised me, thus spurring him to be a passionate and honourable father for our future kids. I loved the moments he shared the most personal and private parts of his life with me. I felt like the trusted keeper of his secrets. I felt like the caretaker of his heart and I wanted to keep it safe and as close to mine as possible.

He let me in to his heart and now he was showing me parts of his soul. He was letting me see scars from his past. And it hurt me to hear about his pain. But I could not help but see the hope in his eyes that the future did not have to reflect that past bleakness. We were in this together now. B1 and B2 taking on the world. He described the type of house he wanted and how big the yard should be. He talked about our home being open to host people and the meals we would cook. He talked about names he liked for a son and the impressive shoe game our kids would have. I kept these conversations close to my heart because I could not believe anyone could love me so much they would actually want to marry me. And I could not believe I would love someone so much that I could not imagine marrying anybody else. *It was him.* My entire world was wrapped up in five feet and eight inches of tattooed hunk. He would wrap his arms around my waist until he could grip his elbows and I was snug against his chest. Then my curious fingertips smoothed the bristles of his beard trickling down to his chest. Right there – that is where I wanted to be forever, nestled in his neck. It was my favourite place. When he held me close like that, and I could feel his heart beating, my problem-prone life faded away and we were just us, having entire conversations with no words. I do not know what it is about physical touch but boy is it an effective communicator! *How do you stop your hands from exploring the one you love? How do you stop the one you love from exploring your body when their touch drives you wild?*

My best friend did not just have my heart, now he had my body and it remembered every sensation. It started to crave him with an intensity that was near impossible to subside. His rugged hands gripped my waist and pulled me close before he traced the outline of my taut torso following the hourglass curve down to fuller hips. And he did it in a tender and thorough way that excited my heartrate and momentarily stole my breath. No one had ever touched me like that. But it did not scare me. I wanted him to discover my body; I would watch his face and listen to his deep breathing and it made me feel like a woman to know that even though he did not say anything I could see he was losing control. He wanted skin to touch. He was already unravelling me in his mind. I felt empowered that my body alone could make him weak and nervous and excited all at the same time. I could feel his heart beat faster the more his hands explored, and my body savoured every moment. We knew we were flirting with a boundary we should have sprinted far away from, but now we were here and the firm thoughts in our heads were overthrown by the magnetic pull of our flesh.

"Brooke, you need to stop! Get in your car and drive away! Now!" said the voice in my head. I lost count of how many times this voice warned, begged and urged me to be strong enough to leave without compromising more of my innocence and purity. But if I was going to be his wife anyway, what is the harm in letting him see, taste and touch the body that would soon belong to him? I loved the fact that he could not say no to me. I quickly became provocative and seductive and altogether impossible to refuse. I studied his face and learned the patterns of pleasure. I loved seeing him almost entirely powerless when I teased him with my body. I was a quick learner and I knew how to make him nervous now. He would present strong and unbreakable, putting up a fight to resist me, but I only licked my lips in acceptance of the challenge and within minutes I wore him down. It was fun and exciting and it felt amazing. His eyes told me he wanted me and his hands told me he could not resist. And I wanted him even more. Soon enough, honouring God was not a priority anymore; getting a hormone-fuelled fix was dominating our actions. Some days we agreed not to see each other because we knew what we would end up doing. Sometimes it worked. But most of the time it did not. He was on my mind all day, every day. My body was addicted to him now and I could feel him in the deepest parts of my soul. How was I supposed to function without him? I have never been addicted to substances but the high I felt with him left me yearning for more. So every time I saw him we went further and further. There was no turning back. Our consciences begged us to make wiser choices, but our bodies refused to be denied pleasure. Relapsing after days or weeks of no intimacy was our new routine. I learned that willpower in the face of temptation is a weak partner; sometimes it does not even bother to leave the house with you when you are headed off to test it out.

I was undone at the smell of his cologne. I was insatiably pleased by his touch. I was confidently lost in his eyes. And I was unmistakably his. My best friend held the other end of a triple knotted soul tie and I was wholeheartedly consumed with us. We were going to be together forever. The only man I was ever intimate with was preparing to marry me. How could I be so lucky? Now it was just a matter of time …

HE LOVES ME NOT

Well, it did not take long for *time* to kill my buzz. And soon the day came that sobered me up and shook me out of my fantasy.

He did not see a future together anymore …

I felt numb. I was not sure if this was happening for real. I sort of froze. Although I may have been trying to process, not much was going through my mind. It was all white noise. I think I probably stopped breathing too. I remember just lying on the floor in my room, then sitting up to feel if my heart was still beating. And suddenly there came the most agonising ache.

I lost.

I just lost everything.

I cried in groans. I sobbed heavy tears; ones that mourned the break of my heart. I do not remember if I stopped crying or if I fell asleep exhausted by the pain. There was not a single part of me that was not consumed by him: my mind, body, heart and soul all ached at once. I know this sounds dramatic, but I honestly thought I was going to die. It hurt that much. Still completely in love with him and, almost without warning, completely cut off. How was I supposed to pick myself back up now?

I felt like I gave him everything I had; every part of me and he dropped it and walked away. A million and one questions swirled through my mind over the next few months of rediscovering myself. *Was I not marriage material after all? Why didn't I listen to that voice in my head? Would I be this broken if I hadn't given him my body? Did he mean it when he said he loved me? Did he mean it when he planned our future? Did he mean it when he said he never wanted to lose me? Am I easily forgotten? Will I ever be able to say I love you to someone without seeing his face? How do I forget his eyes? How do I peel my body off him now? How do I convince myself that I don't need to be insecure about other girls in his life that look like his ex? Was there someone else who lured him away from me? Or did I push him away? Or did he get bored of me and decide I wasn't enough for him? Was he comparing me to the other girls before me? Will he ever give my heart back? Who am I without him?*

The ache that hurt the most was the loss of my best friend. Who did I have now? Although I knew I had people in my life, I felt alone. And I felt broken. He was everywhere. Everywhere I went I had memories with him. Every time my phone pinged I thought it was him. Every time I drove I saw the model of his car, and I would hold my breath checking the number plate, then release a sigh, half disappointed and half relieved that it was not him. I had hoped he would call and say it was all a big mistake and he was sorry and let's start over. Many nights I cried myself to sleep going over every detail in my head of things I could have done differently to keep him in my life. I wished with all my might to wake up and realise it was just a really bad dream and that in reality it was not actually this painful to breathe. I would hear his voice in my head saying his famous parting words every time I was with him, "I love you, Brooke. Don't forget that." Those words used to comfort me and gave me confidence that our future was full of infinite possibilities. But now the same words drove a rusted dagger in my gut, and they replayed over and over in my head as I wept myself to sleep.

It was a fight and a half to stay sane. *Who was going to want me now?* I was not pure and untouched anymore. I felt like damaged goods. I felt abandoned; left with a gaping hole in my chest. I pictured him out there somewhere walking around with my heart and body still wrapped around him. I was an empty shell. I had to retrain myself to not see him as my 'go to' person anymore. And that was the killer. Whenever anything exciting happened, he had been the first to know. Whenever something tragic happened, he had been the first to know. When I was free, we hung out. When I was busy, he called dibs on my spare time. When I was in his arms, he made me feel safe. When I was asleep, he let me know he was thinking of me. I felt like I could no longer function properly. Even though I was good at my job I felt like I was falling apart. I was scared people would start asking about my puffy eyes. And I was scared I would break down if one more person asked me if I was OK. Sometimes I would be driving home when a wave of emotion would blindside me and before I knew it I was balling my eyes out. Some days I missed him so bad I had to purposely leave my phone in a different room so I was not tempted to contact him. How do you tell yourself there will be a day when you do not feel this low, and sound convincing? I wanted to know if he was hurting just as much. I wanted to know if he thought about me every day the way I thought about him. I desperately wanted to know if he missed me or regretted calling it quits or if he even still loved me. But I had to heal. And time had to do its thing.

Really I wanted to hate him. I really did. I wanted to have at him with accusations and insults and conclusions and all the hurtful things I conjured up in my grieving moments. I wanted to inflict the same kind of emotional pain on him that I felt. But I could never bring myself to do it. Because if I did not think I would be able to move forward from this kind of rejection and abandonment, how could I live with the responsibility of hurting someone else like that? The pain was unbearable and healing was torturous, and I would not have wished this even on my worst enemy – no not even on him, my heart's breaker.

And I was sorry. So sorry that I had found myself in his backseat time after time and that we could not take any of it back. Every choice has a consequence and this was a lesson I learned a tremendously painful way. I think the worst part was that I had known I did not have to go down that road to see where it led, but I had done it anyway because my curiosity got the better of me. And to be perfectly honest, I had not wanted to listen to anyone who had my back and advised me not to push boundaries I would later regret violating. I wanted what I wanted. And now I had to face the ramifications of unwise decisions; to deal with intense shame. I had to deal with the guilt of seducing a man who was not my husband and with the insecurities that surfaced now about the person I had become when my desires took over my senses.

So if he was meant to be my future, but now he was gone, what was my future going to look like? I had spent months and months dreaming with him; dreaming of him and all the things we talked about. We talked about our home and our kids and our goals. *What do I do with all of those dreams and hopes now?* He removed himself and not once did I ever consider I might need to have a plan B in case he was not serious. I believed every word he said. Now I did not know what to do. I did not know who to spend my time with now. I did not even really know who I was without him now. I did not know how to move on. I did not know how to let go. I did not know how to look forward to my future if he decided he was not going to be a part of it. *Did I even have a future to look forward to anymore? Or were all my days going to be this painful? How was I supposed to tell my nana that her darling boy she loved so dearly, her favourite pick for her granddaughter, her number one approval, was not going to be with me after all?* They had sat together on a deck and she told him she hoped her granddaughters would marry someone like him. She cried tears of joy when I told her he loved me back. She asked after him every day and told me to send him her love. I was not sure

I could bear the thought of disappointing her. And I might have also been too embarrassed to let her see I was ripped to shreds internally. *How do I save face?*

He changed my life the moment he walked into it, and he changed it the moment he walked out of it. I could not decide if I was the real thing for him or just the warm up routine for all his best lines. He had been on the bench for a little while and maybe it got a little boring there. *Maybe he wanted to get back in the game but needed an ego boost first? Maybe I was just the convenient candidate? Maybe he just wanted to graduate me into the category of people who were no longer relevant in his life?* I wanted answers and closure but the best I got was just that he was not ready. *Great. Where to from here?* It felt like there was not an explanation in the world that would suffice. Have you ever watched an action movie and witnessed the aftermath of an unsuspecting town levelled by an airstrike? And as the camera pans over the ruins, from the rubble crawls the disfigured body of a lone survivor; it zooms in to reveal charred skin, bloody cuts and missing limbs? That was me. What could be worse than being taken out along with everything else in your life? Being the one lonely survivor, processing the devastation around you, and dealing with the overwhelming pain of loss, that is what.

It was inevitable that our paths would cross sooner or later. We were a part of the same circle of friends. *How the heck do you act normal? How the heck do you avoid awkward questions from people who might not actually care about the hurt and just want to know what happened for gossip's sake? How do you attend weddings and not think about what could have been? How do you hold it together when his name comes up in conversation and it is conveniently coupled with someone else? Do I play the game too? Do I try to make myself look like I don't need him? Do I try to desperately line someone else up who looks nothing like him so he can feel insecure about himself? Do I keep wearing the clothes he loved so he burns every time he sees me? Do I post all my highlights, so it looks like I never skipped a beat and he never stopped me from having momentum in life? Do I air all his dirty laundry? Everything he told me in confidence over the years of our friendship, am I still bound by loyalty to keep those things private? Or do I have permission now to be liberally lipped? Do I make his life hell? Do I make him feel uncomfortable, and turn people against him? Do I become his worst nightmare? Do I make sure that if I couldn't have him, no one else could?* This was my daily battlefield. I had unanswered questions, a butt load of conclusions based off my hurt and observations, and I was left with choices. I learned that making the right choices, after a string of wrong choices that felt right at the time, cost me everything. Every ounce of strength I had in me was used to not become a typical ex. And it felt so unfair. It felt like he got away with murder and flashed a grin over his shoulder every now and again to remind me.

But some days I missed him so terribly I could not help crying. *What if he missed me too? What if he was just wearing a brave face too? What if he actually realised he still loved me and still wanted our future together? What if everything in his life was reminding him of me too? What if he was tossing in his sleep, restless at the thought that he made a call that he wished he had never made? What if it was dawning on him that I was the game-changer in his record of dead-end relationships? Should I reach out? Or do I have too much pride to do that? What if I do it and he tells me everything I want to hear? What if I do it and he doesn't tell me everything I want to hear? Could I handle being rejected twice? Brooke, how would you respond if he told you he still loved you? How would you respond if he wanted to try again? Would you fall into his arms? Or would you fight him? Would you argue and pick apart every sentence, scrutinising it with expert precision to avoid believing a lie again? Or do you take him at his word?*

Honestly, I do not think that any of the times when he admitted to still being in love with me were anywhere near as satisfying as I thought they would be. I used to lie awake, running those scenarios through my head and desperately longing to hear him say those words to me. But when it actually happened face-to-face, it was nothing like the movies.

There was no mood lighting and climactic music building in the background. There was no passionate kiss at the end and a 360-degree spinning shot of our reignited love. He did not show up in a tux with a dozen roses, or sprint through airport boarding gates to catch me before I ran away to the other side of the world. He did not shed tears or beg me to take him back. Those words 'I still love you' did not make me feel good. They did not relieve me of my pain. They did not even heal my heart. The hurt was so deep that even though my head wanted to believe he was telling the truth, my trust had been broken. And that overshadowed everything. I already believed him with my whole heart the first time he said those words to me. Then he dropped me so easily, like those words were as mundane as ordering a coffee. And now to say them to me after all that, they lost their power. My love was ruined.

So whilst he re-joined the crew of 'most eligible bachelors with eyelashes any girl would kill to have', I was hiding – too scared my wounds were as obvious as my eye colour. I used to look myself in the mirror and say, "Brooke, you'll never give him credit for breaking your heart, but man he stomped on it real good." I pulled out every half-truth I had to ease my pain. *You are hurt but you're not broken. You are hurt but you're not broken. You are hurt but you're not broken…* Denial became my new bestie and I was not mending anywhere near as thoroughly as I needed to. This delayed my healing and was about as effective as putting a bandaid over a gunshot wound. In other words, it was absolutely hopeless.

I wrestled with whether I should say those words back to him or not. I knew I was staying tight-lipped because of a few things. I did not want to give him the satisfaction of knowing I still loved him too. He could not be allowed to see any sign of weakness because I already felt vulnerable; bleeding out in open deep blue, just waiting for the shark fins to appear. I did not know if I would be able to say those words again, in that context, knowing that my heart was not whole. How do you say 'I love you' and mean it from the bottom of your heart, when your heart is lying at the bottom of a pit, hardly beating? I also did not want to hear myself say it out loud. It hurt too much. The immediate backlash in my head any time those words were said to me after the plummet to the pavement was 'no you don't'. Everything I loved in life now had a bitter aftertaste and I could not escape him in any of the things I used to enjoy. He really did get the best parts of me, didn't he? And now I felt like I had nothing left to offer. Someone conquered me. Someone came and made off with all my most valuable assets. I did not ever think I would have to rebuild my whole person, my whole life and routine, my whole future, from the inside out. From the ground up.

THE F WORD

My bitter stage was ugly. Oh my goodness, it was ugly. It felt good to be angry at someone and then spend hours practicing the mic-drop one-liners you would say to them in the hypothetical confrontations you would have in your head. Ohhh yes, you know what I am talking about. When you are brushing your teeth and admiring your morning hair and almond shaped eyes. Then that little voice inside says, "…And you know what else?!" and your hate-fire flares instantly. There you are with your sassy head movements and arm gestures telling the mirror that he lost the best thing that has ever happened to him – between spits of toothpaste on the vanity! Do not even act like you have not done that. Bitterness is unpleasantly distasteful. The sourness lingers longer than you would like and if you are not careful it can burrow a root in your heart and start growing love-choking weeds in your life. Before you know it, you are not just bitter at one person, you are bitter in general. Bitter towards everyone and everything, although it always leads back to your initial root.

So here I was, a few months into project 'fix-my-broken-heart' and I was aware that bitterness had crept in. I obviously did not want to be that way, but I also did not want to let go of it because projecting blame for pain onto someone else is always easier than dealing with it. I remember I was just starting to sound convincing when people asked if I was OK;

time was doing an average job at healing me. I remember feeling like I had some clear direction about the next season of my life and so I got to work right away. I poured my energy and time into it and I patted myself on the back for how productive I was, considering my emotional turmoil. There was a great opportunity that came up for me and to be honest with you it was a complete answer to prayer. And I was determined to snatch it up to prove to myself that I was still able to be *someone*. I remember having time with God, just praying for wisdom on this opportunity and wanting to be upfront about honouring Him first. If this was not something He wanted me to do, I was not going to do it. It turns out He wanted me to do it. But His condition of entry just about knocked me off my chair …

He pretty much said to me that before I stepped even one foot into this new role, I had to forgive. *Uh, excuse me Sir? No thanks.* At first I thought I heard wrong, so I sipped my tea and carried on. Then it came again and I was super casual at first.

"Yeah ok, Jesus, no problem mate … There's no chance!"

He nudged me again. "God! No way! Come on, You're not seriously asking me to forgive him are you?! Surely, You can make an exception on this one?"

He was silent and I shot at Him again, "God! You saw how broken I was! You saw how much he hurt me! Don't You remember the nights I wept with no words? Just aching groans? Don't You remember?! God, don't make me do it!"

At that moment I felt Him tenderly put just one finger on my heart. He said, "Brookie, please don't act like he doesn't deserve grace and forgiveness … as if you earned yours."

Oh boy! Yep. Knocked right off my chair.

RAIN, RAIN, GO AWAY

I may as well tell you about the time when I had my own personal 'woman at the well' moment. Let's rewind a few months to when I was still freshly wounded. It was raw. I felt exposed. And even worse – I never thought of myself as insecure, but man was I insecure! How do you go from being a future wife to no longer in the picture? I think it would have hurt less to sever my right arm off with a plastic butter knife. I was officially not wanted anymore and my self-worth took a hit I wasn't sure I could bounce back from. The bruising made it hard to breathe. It was like I had run as quickly as my legs could take me down to the bottom floor to get to my pieces on the pavement. And whilst I was desperately trying to recover every little piece, hoping that the damage was not as severe as I feared, a cloud of hopelessness formed above me. And then, like all low points in the movies, it started to rain. It rained hard and I realised that there was no way I could put those pieces back together. So now, I was insecure. *What did I have now?* I had nothing to offer. I had given him my entire heart. *Was there something wrong with me? Could I change it and would that make him want me back?* Did I have a secret expectation that he might come and help me find the pieces? Yes. Did it happen? Nope (c'mon that only happens in movies!). It felt like he tiptoed right over the mess and crossed the road to scope out other towers. *Was my tower not good enough? What did the other towers have that mine did not?* I was definitely insecure.

I cut myself off from a lot of people and kept my circle smaller than small as I nursed my wounds. I had not yet had the courage to have the conversation with my parents about everything that had gone down but when that day came, although it was hard, to my relief it actually freed me. I had been gradually healing but I dared not touch the intense guilt and shame I carried because I knew that part would be messy and painful. So, you could say I really only aired my wounds out enough for them to scab over – surface-level healing. I had spent the majority of the day crying and working up as much bravery as I could manage to tell my dad how dishonest I had been, and then to confess how broken I was now. We sat on the lounge, just us two, and I slowly began to tell my dad about my broken pieces. I sobbed and he listened. I was trying to be so brave but inside I felt like my head hung low – I was such a screwup and I was not worthy of my dad's compassion, especially after betraying his trust. I knew my decisions had lead me there and I felt the full weight of the consequences. I knew I deserved them.

I poured my heart out to him about my first love and how ruined I was. I sobbed, "Dad, he was the first boy I ever loved!" He was the first of many things for me and I began listing them. "He was my first kiss … He was the first hand I ever held …"

What happened next forever changed me. My dad graciously interrupted me in the gentlest way and said, "No, I was the first hand you ever held." I cannot tell you what that one truth did for me internally. I felt like it was the moment my parched soul received living water at the well. That one truth put my pity-party on pause and reminded me that I was a daughter before I was a lover, and my worth to my dad had not changed even though I was rejected by someone else. I saw myself as hunched-over damaged goods, but I was reminded in a whisper, "Chin up, baby girl, don't forget I am your first love."

Those were my words of living water. Words I will not trade-in for the rest of my life.

In that moment I felt restored. I had been so embarrassed that I did not have my love anymore. I had been so ashamed that I crossed boundaries I should have protected. I had been hanging my head internally, crushed by the disappointment. And yet here I was being validated and reminded of how loved

I am by my dad. It liberated me from the cloud of pain that hung heavy on me. But the reality was that time still needed to heal my heart and I needed a new perspective for my future. Not only that, I had to work intentionally at choosing forgiveness every day. Diary, it was such a hard place to be. I remember some days just sitting in my car crying because I still had a sore heart and I did not feel like being brave.

I had never been more desperate to run away and heal without constant reminders of my pain in my face every day … So, I boarded a plane to Canada; all too eager to leave a painful reality behind. I was headed for a winter wonderland in hopes that I might just get a brand-new heart for Christmas.

WIDE OPEN SPACES

Kristen and I drove through a township called Niagara on the Lake. It was one of the most beautiful places I had ever seen. Acres and acres of snow-covered vineyard running alongside a vast lake of deep blue, not entirely frozen over. Big old country barns, lone standing, with snow-capped roofs housing harvest. Cosy homesteads were tucked away behind white-dusted pines. If I close my eyes, I can still smell the sweet aroma of the Rocky Mountain Chocolate Factory we stopped in to visit. I can still feel the frost smack my cheeks numb. I can still feel the icicles in my nostrils defrost as we blasted the heater. A few nights later we were driving past farmland in New Market and there it was … Wide open spaces to scan and dream. Hills that rose and fell between winding tracks ploughed at dawn. The warm glow of Christmas lights lining frames like gingerbread houses. Before I knew it, we were flying across country to Edmonton and yep, you guessed it, more and more expanse to marvel at. A grid of brown land covered with snow like a fresh icing-dusted batch of brownies.

A few weeks later I was in country Ohio. Coshocton was the name of the little county with rolling hills and stretches of farmland covered in snow. Ponds were frozen over and the locals skated carefree. We trekked in ankle deep snow into the woods to shoot at hunting targets and the trees stood tall as the wind whistled and chilled every bone in our bodies. We visited family farms and manors in Butler, Pittsburgh and drank hot apple cider and followed deer tracks into the forest.

PROMISES & PERSPECTIVES

About a month after leaving Sydney for Canada I found myself standing in the middle of a swap meet in Compton, Los Angeles. Across from me stood a deeply respected life mentor of mine (and self-appointed older sister), Niyah is her name. And when she shoots straight, Niyah brings the fire. She was making me cry, like only a big sister can, as she lovingly told me not to let my trip go to waste by returning to Sydney fearful of suffocating again. Of course, she did it with her classic ghettos of Brooklyn, New York charm.

"Brooke, quit walking around like you got a limp just 'cos you got your heart broken. You go back to Sydney and you walk. Everything God has shown you is to give you foresight for the year ahead. You're not broken anymore. Walk."

She was right. God had shown me more than enough to walk confidently, knowing that no matter what I returned home to, there was hope and wholeness waiting ahead. I guess I just needed a passionate New Yorker to remind me.

I can say this and mean it with all that I have in me, I am grateful that I went through that heartbreak. I never thought I would get to a place where I could see the good that came out of it, but I do not think we would have much of a story if not. The truth is this – heartbreak led me back to my God. My heart wandered away from Him and the pain of it being broken drew me closer than I was before. How thoroughly He sifted through the layers of hurt, I could never express with enough gratitude. If He had not bothered with it, I would still be stuck in a pit of despair. He kept His watchful eye on me as I healed and then He loved me to wholeness. I never thought there would come a day that I could think of the person who broke my heart and not feel the pain. I never thought I could get to a place where I had forgiven him completely. I never thought I could genuinely pray the best for him and his future.

Diary, it almost seems a bit unfair to be brave when your heart is broken. On one hand you want to be left to lick your wounds in peace, but on the other you kind of want to stick it to the person who hurt you and show them you are still standing. I think I have learned that being brave is not ignoring hurt; I think being brave is defined by facing the things that hurt us the most. It surprised me how much I was challenged to be brave whenever I thought about my future. I do not even really know if there is a right or wrong way to do it. It might just be the fact that we choose bravery over brokenness that determines what our next chapter looks like.

Love,

B xx

VI

TAKE HEART

I have told you these things, so that in me you
may have peace. In this world you will have trouble.
But take heart! I have overcome the world.

John 16:33

Dear Diary,

What's in it for the UN-BRAVE?

I am certain I am not the only one who has asked myself or God or a confidante this question: "Why do bad things happen to good people?" We have all asked that question, haven't we? I have asked it when something has happened in life that caused the very ground beneath me to shake. I have asked it when my mind could not logically explain the reason for a blindsided attack or surprise ambush. What about when a savage blow winded me so severely that I was rolling on the floor, unsure I could take another breath? Between you and I, Diary, this is the question I have asked God when I have doubted Him entirely. When I doubt His existence and everything I have learned or experienced of Him in my life.

I had a conversation with Him once when He taught me some things. I asked Him, "God, why do bad things happen to good people?" and I felt like He answered me with a question (classic God).

"Brooke, what or who do you consider to be good?"

Okay, I am not gonna lie, I kind of felt like this was a trick question so I took my time answering it. I just wanted to let the suspense build, y'know! Actually, I was frantically wracking my brain for an intelligent answer! I made a list in my head of all the things in this world I saw as *good*. And all the kinds of people I categorised as *good* versus *not that good* and even *not good at all*. As I happily ordered my lists, I felt like He peered over my thoughts and then gently tapped my shoulder to pause for a second. I looked up and He said, "I'm good." I was about to scribble through the first name on my *good* list and add His, but I knew He was not finished.

"…And you live in a fallen world."

Oh.

Well Diary, it is kind of obvious that perhaps we should have called it quits a long time ago, when life dealt us a crummy hand. We should have thrown in the towel and opted out, because who wants to live a life of uncomfortable faith, right? Who wants to persevere through pain and grit and heartache? Who wants to get up and fight a battle you literally have to trust God to win on your behalf? Who wants to feel the full force of an enemy attack and cling to faith for dear life? Seriously, who wants to be known as the 'Job family'? Job lost everything! But he also never surrendered his faith.

I have been wondering if faith and bravery are linked. They might just be synonymous with each other. They might just be the gears we shift between to keep momentum in this life of roadblocks and detours. I can't deny that there have been very real moments of throwing my hands up at God and screaming,

"What are you doing to us?! This isn't fair!" And He has let me have my bratty moment, before He has calmed me and shown me how much He has been at work. I can say that there is nothing glamorous about being the 'Job family' but if my life of walking by faith so far has taught me anything, it would be that it is an honour. It is an honour to be the ones He uses to show His glory. It is an honour to be chosen as the family who refuses to denounce our loyalty to Him. It is an honour to pave paths for others to follow back to Jesus. We know that He is for us. We know that He who began a good work within us will be faithful to bring it to completion. We know that He closely attends to the prayers of God-loyal people.

I have been learning that the *greater plan* holds so much power when I am not consumed with my own mini stories. What I mean is that the only way I can live brave, and give others permission to live brave, is to have faith that better days are ahead. Maybe that is the whole challenge though. Diary, I have been thinking about how my life reads to others. I have been thinking about how profound my impact is on people who would consider me brave and themselves not. I have been wondering what the purpose of perseverance is. And why etched in the spirit of humanity is a desperate longing for hope and reassurance that being subjected to fickle flesh is not all that there is to this life. I have been wondering if holding onto faith is really worth it this side of eternity. I think it is Diary. I think that in the same way I have watched the lives of those who have inspired me to keep going, there could be others watching mine. And what if they are feeling un-brave? What if they are looking for someone who has walked the path before and can guide them along it? What if they are waiting for me to make it out the other side so they have hope and confidence that they can make it too? What if they are hanging onto their faith by a thread and my Job-resolve keeps them trusting God for yet another day?

BRAVERY FOR THE DAY & NIGHT

I know that whenever I was overcome with fear from the nightmares there were a few internal thoughts that ran around in my head. *Is God real? If He is why isn't He protecting me? Does God want me to be scared? If not, why can't I sleep? Did I do something bad to deserve bad dreams? If so, how do I fix it? Does God really love me? If so why does He let me cry all the time?* These thoughts and questions swam in my mind and heart every time I found myself wide-eyed and alert in the eerie dead of night. I could not wait for morning's first light because that meant I had survived the shadows and they could not scare me while the sun was up.

At the foot of my bed stands a sword. Our family started a tradition that every child receives a sword for their 21st birthday. So far, my big sis' The Rose has one, I have one, and now my younger sister has one too. The tradition is we each have a few weeks to search for our sword design online, or have a day of sword-shopping with Mum and Dad. Once we have picked our sword, my parents buy it and engrave it with our 'life verse'. This verse is the scripture that we choose to live by. My sword is like the one from Brave Heart and is engraved with Ephesians 4:16 – 'Robust in Love'.

> We take our lead from Christ, who is the source of everything we do. He keeps us in step with each other. His very breath and blood flow through us, nourishing us so that we will grow up healthy in God, *robust in love.*
>
> – Ephesians 4:16 The Message (emphasis added).

I love this tradition because it speaks volumes of our family's firm foundation. But more than that I believe it is a powerful declaration. I see it as my parents giving us permission to join the battle field of life – armed. In our Pacific Islander culture, the 21st birthday is a momentous celebration where you are given a blessing from your family and official recognition as an adult; now in charge of your own life. Freedom at last! Traditionally, you are presented with an elaborate key, usually the length of your arm and custom carved or ordered. The key is symbolic of your freedom and the key to life.

I am grateful that my parents have always chosen to set a Godly standard for our family. Honouring Him has been the only thing that has kept our family together. It is the only thing that has kept us going, and it will be the only thing that spurs us onward and will sustain us till the end. My parents have always taught us kids how to recognise the schemes of darkness whenever a hard season has come our way, and by the handful of stories I have selected to share with you, it is obvious there is a target on our backs as a family. I wonder if that is what my dream about Cry means. These days the only dreams that get my heart racing are the ones that involve my big sister. Yes, we are still in the fight for her and for our family to be whole again. Every day that I wake up, my sword reminds me I am in the fight.

Every night that I sleep, my sword stands guard. Every time fear wakes me, my sword is within arm's reach to remind darkness that I fight for light. My sword represents the Truth of His Word. And His Word says the Truth sets you free. That is true freedom. (Thanks Mum and Dad.)

BRAVERY TO STAY

A little while back I sat in the office of a cardiologist. He attempted to reassure me that he would do everything to ensure my heart was going to make a full recovery from some scary episodes that had seen me rushed to hospital a couple of times. As he screened me and explained the extensive testing I would undergo over the next month, he said some profound words that had my mum and I wink at each other with confidence. He said, "Brooke, you have trained your heart well, I am sure you will make a full recovery." He was right. I have trained my heart well. It knows the Word of God is my sure foundation. It has been trained to trust Him. It has been trained to cling to Him no matter what. It has been trained to hold onto His promises even if it is physically struggling to beat.

The crappiest year of my life gave me more than enough opportunities to give up. It gave me many chances to let my heart become bitter or grow cold or remain defeated, because my life looked nothing close to being filled with hope and joy. But Diary, I have come to realise that when I walk out in my faith and wear my brave, it becomes increasingly obvious that my resilience is sharpened and so too with it my ability to stay grounded is remarkably cemented, even when all the things I find security in are shaken.

BRAVERY FOR THE ROSE

Diary, how do you encourage others to stay strong and hang in there even when you have not seen the miracle in your own life yet? I have been wandering if this part of the process is actually more critically impacting than the celebration at the end. I kind of think it is. I hate to admit it but I am starting to understand that being brave enough to trust the process is just as powerful as receiving the miracle or answer to prayer. I am fervently praying that that is the testimony of my sister when she returns home. I have been fighting to stand firm on the promises that my God is in all the details of our lives; as messed up as they are. I think this is what brave looks like: I am my sister's keeper.

BRAVERY IN THE DETAILS

I do not think I have had much of a choice but to become aware that pain has a way of causing me to shut down, or retreat into a dark place within. Heartbreak has a way of building impenetrable walls and pooping all over my ability to trust. I have become aware that grief has a way of hanging sorrow over me like a wet blanket and holding me for what feels like an eternity before I see even a glimmer of hope that better days are ahead. I am also now aware that shame has a cruel way of hanging my head and banishing me to a dark corner of disqualification from any and all things good.

Diary, I have to admit it is hard to take God at His word sometimes. Well, let's be honest, most times. My untamed heart and selfish nature lead me astray and my flesh bears the brunt of the devastation. But having faith in the Unseen and fearing the unknown leaves me suspended in this uncomfortable tension. It is the tension between heart and mind; the tension between flesh and spirit; the tension between right and wrong; the tension between the promise and the mean time. It is a hard place to be. But what if being brave was as simple as playing a role in a scene, with the knowledge that there is still the rest of the movie to be filmed? What if the scene I am currently in actually is not the end, even though it feels like it is crushing me? What if the Director is holding the script with a smile because triumph is but a scene away? Can I commit to seeing this scene through, and look forward with hope, knowing the details rest in the hands of a Skilful Director?

BRAVERY FOR A RENEWED HEART

I was stubborn and squirming as God was pruning me on my forgiveness journey. After fighting Him on my willingness to forgive, I finally waved the white flag and decided to be obedient. But I had to choose forgiveness every day; because every day there was a reminder or a new reason to go back on my word. He made it clear that it was not enough for my broken heart to be restored, it had to be renewed. He could see me suffocating and He was kind enough to give me wide open spaces. I needed a shift in my perspective. My heart wanted the castle and I was determined to stay with Him. But my eyes could only see the dirt patch and seemingly stagnant progress. I needed to know that He was still at work behind the scenes and that He was going to give me hope every time I hit a road block. That He was going to give me a promise to cling to every time I was tempted to get discouraged; every time I did not realise my guard had slipped and my heart took another hit; every time I cried in my car because that day I did not feel like being 'Brooke the Brave'. He was with me every time I felt the sting as He pruned and refined me.

Diary, in my moments of trusting God in this healing process I felt like He began painting a stunning self-portrait as a King; as the ultimate keeper of hearts. He was nobility that tended carefully to broken things and could be trusted with no semblance of doubt. His wax seal love was final. The seal of the King was impressed on my heart and I had to trust that He knew what He was doing. I just had to obey Him. He was pouring wisdom into my heart and as I chose to linger with Him every day – not in a hurry to leave His presence – He was helping me forgive. He was reminding me that bitterness is not found in *robust love*. And that I received His love, grace, kindness and forgiveness freely, so I do not get to be selective about whom to extend all of those same things to. He was renewing me.

Does forgiving count as bravery? I feel like of all the uncomfortable situations I have been through in life, forgiving has seemed the most impossible to do. But I wonder if that is why it takes every bit of brave that I have. I wonder if when I am brave enough to forgive and be renewed, I might just be free enough to live a life with restored joy.

* * *

WHAT IS BRAVERY?

Can it take many forms? Is it an action or an attitude or an attribute? Does bravery always present itself in the eleventh hour, when we find ourselves scrambling for every last ounce of courage we have hidden inside our hearts? Or is it a premeditated response to situations we desperately wish to avoid? Does it always feel like sucking in ice cold air, in deep breaths, attempting to ease a rapidly thudding heart? Or does it feel like a girding suit of armour, offering protection in a bloody battle, thus persuading us to join the war?

Does bravery always guarantee a victorious outcome?

What things warrant bravery?

Do we weigh up each scenario and make a split-second decision about whether bravery is required? Or is it a daily choice, as routine as brushing our teeth? Is bravery ever something we just have for ourselves? Or in typical brave fashion, does it always speak volumes of inspiration to the onlookers, the by-standers, the life-observers, the integrity-scrutinisers, the hardship-spectators, the passively opinionated? The un-brave?

Does bravery always leave a pregnant pause in the bravee's story during the reader's intermission? Does bravery promise a next chapter? A better one? A plot twist or alternative ending to the story? Is it possible that when we choose to be brave, we unknowingly tweak the theme of upcoming chapters and create a new story within the story?

It quite possibly could be all of the above.

If my life is a story that I fervently pray always points people to Jesus, let it be said that I live it bravely.

Take heart, He has conquered the world.

Love,

B xx

VII

ROBUST IN LOVE

We take our lead from Christ, who is the
source of everything we do. He keeps us in step
with each other. His very breath and blood flow
through us, nourishing us so that we will grow up
healthy in God, robust in love.

Ephesians 4:16

What does LOVE look like?

It is a good question, hey Diary? Does anyone really have the answer? I have been thinking that maybe there is something being refined in me through all these things that have demanded my bravery so far …

Do you remember when life seemed pretty cruisy? I would have been about fifteen years old and feeling fairly content with life. We had moved into a new house, I was acing my grades (I am a self-confessed over-achiever and suffer from classic middle child syndrome, a.k.a. 'I am attention-seeking and disgustingly competitive), my friends seemed to be drama free, and my touch footy team had a hot coach and we were smoking other teams (tastefully, of course). All was well in the world and in my fifteen-year-old mentality there was not a whole bunch of urgency for me to grow spiritually because nothing was necessarily 'wrong'. Gosh! A lot of life has happened since then! I remember reading my Bible one morning before leaving to catch the bus to school and being absolutely arrested. I was reading Ephesians 4 that talks about the strength of the Body of Christ as it grows and matures in its faith. At the time I was convinced The Message paraphrase was the most anointed Bible version to read, and I guess for the words that marked me so heavily, I was right.

Ephesians 4:16 describes the body (the collective believers of Jesus) as 'robust in love' in the context of spiritual maturity. Like a burning iron brands cattle, I felt these words singe my heart to its core. I almost could not breathe. It hit me so square in the face. How could love (pure, delicate and innocent love) be described in such a rugged and heavy-armed way? Did I miss something? Was I caught up in the comfort of my small worldly measured success that I fell into the trap of thinking love was not broad shouldered?

Love.

But not just love; *robust* love. As in, a constant pursuit of maturity in faith that is evidenced by love that grows robust. Wow.

I do not know if it is just me, but I certainly do not have a default setting that is OK to love even when it hurts. In fact, my default setting for extending love is very conditional. It is also subject to change. Not necessarily available upon request. And while we are here you may as well read the fine print in the T's and C's too.

What do you mean love wants me to wear it in every context, in every season, in front of every person I encounter? I was convicted. I chewed on these words for weeks. It did not make sense.

ROBUST IN LOVE

Words shape. And in all transparency these three little words with magnified implications SHOOK me. They unsettled me. They shone a spotlight on the condition of my heart and challenged the 'truth' I believed about love. Is it all romantic and fantasised? Is it always sweet-tasting and candle-lit? Does it always look like fairy-tale 'I do's' and passionate scenes in movies I had to cover my eyes for when I was a kid? Or is love more than that?

Maybe love is a *choice*.

Love is the most powerful force of emotion that moves one to action. It is more powerful than hate or anger or jealousy or pride. But maybe sometimes life forces me to settle for warped perceptions of it. Could it be that the fog of oblivion I chose to see love through portrayed it to be soft and mushy and limited to the ever-fleeting satisfaction of feelings? What if love doubled as a bold, unswerving choice to *be* love, or *extend* love, irrespective of feelings?

Robust. What a deeply satisfying word. I cannot help but picture a strong man; a robust man with a stance that is not easily moved. If love is a choice, I have to be militant about it, right? It is repetitive. It is routine. It is a constant happening. It is a discipline. It is refined. It is laboured on and worked at and becomes second nature; much like a soldier marching in time, or diligently making his bed with hospital corners, or shooting every target with precision as he has been trained to do. I can respect and admire a soldier for his discipline and service, but what about the unglamorous things? If I spoke to him face-to-face and asked if he believed even the ugly parts of his job were worth it, what would he say? Would he act surprised because he was unaware there would be traumatic scenarios he might encounter? Or would he confidently smile back at me and say, "Of course it's worth it, that's why I chose it"?

Maybe that is what it looks like, Diary. A well-trained heart, much like a well-trained soldier is fit for battle. It is well-equipped to defeat enemies and win wars and to brave the prospect of certain death. It knowingly enters guaranteed danger zones with confidence that it has trained for every possible outcome. I can't help but feel grateful for being brought up in a family and household that firmly stands on faith in God. Because if I am being entirely honest, without this there is no way growing 'robust in love' is possible, let alone bravely navigating the brutal blows of life.

Everything about these three words challenges the life out of me. I have to choose to live it every day, and I have to resolve that it will always be worth it. I am aware that being all of twenty-four years I still have much to learn in the way of life and love. And please do not mistake me for another keyboard-happy-Gen-Y-life-guru. I am passionate about this topic because I have been challenged to live by it. I would like to say that I chose it to be the most easily identifiable quality or character trait about my life. But if I can be really frank, I am naturally a very selfish person. And sacrificing for the sake of love sounds all gooey and romantic, but honestly it also sounds like it requires character and growth, accompanied by near constant discomfort, maybe even years of uncomfortable scenarios and life interruptions. It sounds like one might require an entire suit of armour made of bravery just to survive. It does not sound too appealing to me. So then, how did I arrive at this decision?

It chose me.

Maybe Love is a *Person*.

I am a Christian. I believe in Jesus Christ. I believe He died on the cross for my sin and I believe He rose again. I also believe that if I have any chance of walking out this life in a manner that inspires others, there is absolutely no way I can do it without Him; my God. I have come to realise that this life is much too painful to try and live without the hope He gives. And maybe, just maybe, the only reason my life has been full of devastating circumstances so far, is because I need to test how solid my faith really is. And maybe He might want to refine in me the kind of 'robust love' He intends to define His matured believers by. I think maybe my spiritual immaturity caused me to think that, with such a 'Mighty God' on my side, I might be immune to life's heartaches. Ha! Yeah, no. Diary, I think I am starting to see that maybe the whole point of believing in a God who is infinitely and immeasurably powerful actually gives me an alternative way to handle the same heartaches everyone else is enduring in this journey called life.

I can't deny how present He has been in every ache I have been through so far. I also can't deny how everything I have written about has solidified another layer of conviction about Who my God is and whether I can actually trust Him with the details of my life. I think it might even be pointless to have the type of faith that only believes in a God of good times and throne-dwelling, far from my unglamorous mess here on Earth. Maybe that is why He chose to sacrifice His Love for me? And all I have to do is choose to navigate life His way; I am guaranteed to come out the other side looking more and more robust in love. If my life so far is just a collection of stories that points to His goodness, then at least I have hope that no matter what lies ahead on my path, He will sustain me. He will walk with me and continue to refine me. Could that be the whole point, Diary? My faith does not just give me somewhere to be for an hour or so on a Sunday (I think that is probably the easiest part of my faith, if I am honest). The real test of its legitimacy is how I live every other day of the week; clinging to the God that I sing songs about trusting with my whole heart. Maybe my faith is not legitimate until I have chosen it to be my steadfast foundation when my entire life is falling apart.

He is so kind in the way that He counsels. I know for certain that it has taken absolute grit for me to commit to this bold by-product of spiritual maturity. There have been many, many, MANY opportunities over the years, since being entrusted with this revelation, for me to either exercise robust love or neglect it. Every single time my default setting justified neglecting it, but every single time the grace-giving wise counsel of His Spirit never let me forget that He has already unpacked it for me, and I have a choice. He has lovingly nudged me when I hated my grandfather for returning to prison, or when I wanted to ignore my dad for betraying my mum, or when my heart was broken, or when my big sister abruptly left our family to write a colourful prodigal son testimony. And in each of these moments He let me wrestle with Him. But every single time He has reminded me that He has called me to be robust in love. He lovingly says, "Brookie, you can't un-know what I have already branded your heart with."

All I know is that He took me by the hand and has been teaching me more about the kind of Love He is. And the kind of love He gives. And when I get to see those parts of Him it makes me want to be more like Him. It makes me want to love like that. It makes me want to be *robust in love*. There are some things that I have found to be true of my fickle heart and His love.

* * *

*There is nothing like the beautiful way He
restores shattered hearts. The ones
mishandled by a rough grip. The ones
mindlessly ditched in flight. The ones
falsely guided to dead-end streets, lined
with shacks of selfishness. The ones that
feel like tampered goods. The ones that
cease beating between gnashing teeth,
wailing groans, knee-worn carpet and
anguish-infused tears.*

*His love is perfectly wholesome;
It tells me I lack nothing.*

*His love is like a full moon,
Gloriously mysterious.*

*His love is pure –
It's incomparably refined.*

*Sometimes my dotted heart forgets that it
is native to His love;
Sometimes it's lured by half-truths and
empty promises,
It's enticed by honeyed flattery.*

*Sometimes it's inconstant,
Sometimes it's compromising,
Sometimes it's unwitting and
Sometimes it's unshielded.*

But what I have found to be true of hearts
is how profoundly they feel the rawness of
loss.

How carelessly they twirl around a fire and
snatch in retreat when licked by the flame.

How sturdy they fortify their walls,
determined to never be accessible.

How loosely they partner with time to heal
the wound.

His love is loyal and secure;
It establishes itself in my heart,
I never have to compete for His attention
or affection.

His love is full and without reservation,
Nothing is withheld from me.

His love is fierce,
It's a mighty oak with deep dug roots.

When my finite capacity to love meets His
infinity, my raindrop heart is fully
encompassed by His ocean –
I am entirely immersed,
Awash with His fullness.

His love steadied me,
It reminded me who I am.

His love freed me,
It gave me permission to live.

His love is perfectly wholesome.

Diary, if the painful things in my life were only catalysts for a deeper revelation of my God, then it is well worth it. I want to be His. I want to live a life that fights for love, because Love fought for me.

I want to be Robust in Love.

Love,

B xx

EPILOGUE –

THE INVITATION

I could not ignore the internal beckoning to ensure I did not conclude this book without as much as an invitation to know Him; my God. His ears are inclined to listen to the desperate prayers of honest hearts. And He promises to closely attend to those loyal to Him.

My prayer has been that throughout this book you have been made aware of an inward yearning; a calling from deep within to reunite your spirit with wholeness. This would be the dwelling of eternity written upon your heart. The Gentleman of your heart will not take it by force. He will wait until you invite Him in. And when He comes, He will stir waters deep within your spirit; an edification beyond the aches of your heart and longings of your soul.

He is the ultimate Keeper of hearts. You can trust Him. If mending and healing are His specialty, would you trust Him to redefine love for you? Would you trust Him to restore hope, joy and peace? For the split second that you are entertaining this thought, I am aware that doubt and disqualification are whispering lies in your ear. Silence them.

He is the God over all. And He has seen every minute detail in the story of your life. Your details do not escape Him. They do not escape His love and forgiveness. Your brokenness does not repel Him. He is drawn to you. I think the best thing about being broken is this simple truth: brokenness qualifies you for redemptive healing.

So dear friend, whom I have entrusted with the pages of my documented brokenness, if you are at your lowest and most broken … what do you have to lose?

Below is a prayer. A prayer I have prayed and sobbed through. It is a prayer that only has power when coupled with your confession and sincerity of heart. Maybe you want to pray it too?

Hi Keeper, it's me,

Here it is. My heart. It is bruised and fractured but it is Yours now. I am choosing to place my heart in Your trustworthy hands and allowing You to mend it like only You can. You designed it in the first place, so I trust that You know where all these broken pieces go. Lord, I am not just asking for a restored heart, I am asking for a renewed heart; a heart that has a fresh revelation of Your love for me and an enlarged capacity to love others like that. I am inviting You to weave Your character into me, sync my heartbeat to Yours, heal the wounds and remove the thorns. I am asking You to rid my heart of lingering hurts and bitterness; breathe freshness into the dusty corners and seal it with the blood You shed on the cross for my freedom.

Thank You for loving me too much to leave me in my shattered state. Thank You that in You I am made whole and I am forgiven.

My heart is Yours. Make it Your home.

In the Name of Jesus, I believe.

Amen.

ACKNOWLEDGEMENTS

God

Without You I have nothing. You have become more real, more accessible and more intimate with me than ever throughout this entire writing and healing journey. Thank You for sitting with me as I typed and cried my way through this project. Thank You for keeping me close to Your heart and being patient with me as I learned how to be vulnerable. Thank You for gifting me with friends who kept me sharp and kept me on the straight and narrow to see this through. Thank You for not giving up on me when I wanted to quit, many times over. Thank You for using my broken pieces to prove Your faithfulness. Gaining intimacy with You is the most precious thing I have this side of eternity and it will forever be my most passionate pursuit. I love You and I am staying with You.

Family

To Mum, Dad and siblings (The Rose, Gabe and J) I love you all. This has been a huge investment in healing for us all and I honour you guys for doing this with me. Thank you for releasing me to tell our story. Thank you for having my back through every ebb and flow of producing something so raw. Thank you for believing in the power of the written word and for choosing to be transparent as a unit. This book and story is a testament to the faithfulness of God and His hand on our family. *Ou te alofa I lou aiga.*

Shana McKibben

You are the greatest editor! I am so blessed to work with you. Thank you for being a safe place for me and for treating this book with as much care and caution as I have. You did not have to take on my manuscript, but you did and I am so grateful you did. It was a huge step for me personally to entrust this to anyone, but you made a time-consuming and tedious process thoroughly enjoyable. Thank you for your encouragement and reassurance. Thank you for your honesty and professionalism. Thank you for believing in me.

Claire Stanmore

Flipping heck! You are my special gift of a friend! You have been present at every point of this journey and you have seen every side. I would not have survived without your consistent friendship. Thank you for loving me through weeping winters as I insisted on becoming a hermit crab, bringing this story to the surface. Thank you for whisking me away to wide open spaces to feed my soul and recalibrate every time I was in a raw state as this project was being refined. Thank you for covering me in prayer and always having a word of encouragement in your heart to refuel me and realign my perspective. The kindness of God … that is what your friendship represents to me. I love you.

Sarah (Wellham) Brouwer

My soul sis. No one's prophetic words have impacted me so profoundly, the way yours have. You have been pure and true and full of love and grace. Thank you for being 'home' for me. You have been in my corner since the beginning. You have been my Spirit-led moral compass through many, many seasons of life and I will forever get emotional when I think about your loyalty and how valuable you are to me. Outside of obedience to God, being brave enough to write this book is because you have been adamant and unapologetic in supporting me living an unconventional life from a place of conviction. "You're not crazy sis,"– four of the most dangerously releasing and equally terrifying words you have ever said to me. You live in my soul, Ser. I love you with a fire.

Bonnie Tan

Oh my Bon … you are a precious friend to me! You were a literal shield for me during the majority of the heartaches that make up this book. You befriended a very broken Brooke. And you protected my vulnerabilities. You were a lifeline and made work bearable, as every day I put on a brave face after sobbing in my car before my shift started. Thank you for being a loyal sounding-board and a safe place for me to process a lot of ugly details and emotions. Thank you for opening your home to me. And thank you for being like a big sister to me during a mass exodus of significant relationships from my life. Thank you for the many prayers you prayed and the many baked goods we shared – what a time! I love you very much, Bon!

Saacha Bear

My little sister!! I am so proud of you. This book is partly your fault. You told me to write it. You took me to your university and threw me in the deep end at 'the chopshop'. You taught me how to receive feedback and how to welcome refinement as a writer. What you may not have known was that at that time I was anxiously awaiting feedback on my first draft. You taught me about the importance of finding my voice as a writer. You sat with me and took notes on experimental writers and you have been such an encouragement to me. You, plus me, plus words, equals a very good and very geeky time! I love you Saach!

Monica Samuel

My friend! You keep me sharp! You keep me laughing! You keep me learning! Thank you for making me more intentional overall. I have become a student of life because of the way you challenge me. I must credit my excessive book reading and tea drinking to you. Thank you for always being a voice of steadfast encouragement and reassurance to me. Thank you for being enthusiastic about every stage of writing this book. And thank you for being a true friend to me in my least honourable moments. You were the first to water and tend to integrity in my life and you committed to seeing the best in me, even as I crawled my way through a comeback. You are a golden friend to me and one I am ever so grateful for. I love you, Mon!

Shivneel Kumar

My brother! Wow, what a journey of discovery and growing in trust and creativity. Thank you for making me laugh until I want to wee my pants. Thank you for believing in this book and being loyal to motivate me however you could. Thank you for raising me in my creativity and being passionate about chasing Jesus, it has kept me in check. Thank you for filling the gap as a sibling when I was feeling stretched beyond my capacity. You brought an element of joy to our home and family that was withering away. For you, I am insanely grateful! I love you, smelly Nelly xx.

Girl squad – Scottie, Michal, Sienna, Nevaeh, Amelia

When you little girls grow up, I hope you will be able to understand how significantly you all impacted my life. Writing this book was a long process. It was a huge investment physically and emotionally. And as I embarked on this adventure I found myself surrounded by a solid girl squad of two-year-olds. Each of you at one point or another was entrusted to me and I was given the honour to be a part of your lives. The truth is you girls have changed my life and my perspective. You girls soften my hardened heart. You girls have taught me what it looks like to have child-like faith, strategically during a period of not having any control over my life and trusting God as I stepped out in faith to apply myself to something I had never done before. You girls became motivation for me to live differently, for the sake of legacy. Thank you for all the cuddles and kisses and the purity of your hearts. My prayer is that each of you grows up to be the kind of girls who know the Person of Love for yourselves and exemplify Him with purity, grace and kindness. Aunty B/Brookie/Sugar Booger/NaNa will always keep you girls close to my heart. Love you all xx.

Karen Brink

My writing buddy!! Being friends with you stirred so much in me that I did not know was there. Whenever we get together or collaborate on creative projects you draw on words from a deep well within me and then you bring ridiculously stunning visual and musical expression to them. Thank you for giving 2D words wings. Whether it is books, poems or songs it is undeniable that you have brought to the surface a deposit of creativity I was unaware of. I will always be grateful for you, the peace you bring to me and the timely words you have seeded, "Never get low or realistic on your dream scale." Okay, friend. Let's do it! I love you dearly, Karen! (And thank you for making an epic book trailer!)

Karla Moors

What a blessing you have been. Thank you for being my writing mentor through all my horrible drafts. Thank you for believing in this book and for pushing me beyond my comfort zone. You made me put on my big girl panties every time you returned feedback. Thank you for being thorough and explaining the importance of vulnerability to me. Thank you for the FaceTimes and phone calls even as you were carting kids to appointments and cooking dinner. You drew emotion out of me and forced me to deal with things I still wanted to hide behind. You gave me a one-on-one lesson about connecting with others and thinking outside of myself rather than trying to save face. You set me up for a win, not just in completing this book but in life. Thank you for teaching me a valuable life principle; it has been validated by oceans of tears and wounds that turned to scars. This book would not have been possible without you.

Josh Crow

Whether you knew it or not you were the neutral conscience by which I filtered some of my most vulnerable details. You were one of the first to water my writing journey with encouragement, even as I wrestled with my own insecurities. As I wrote I often found myself asking, "What would Josh say if he read this?" This is because you have never shied away from telling me the truth; you even risk offending me in the moment for the sake of bringing out the best in me, and that is the way you have always treated me. You are a real one. I will never forget the time and wisdom you have invested in me, especially in the thick of my compromise. I am grateful that you taught me how to choose honour, integrity and value. You have my respect, big bro. Thank you.

Emilio Bonilla

E! If ever there was an individual who forced me to grow, sharpen my revelations and remain teachable by gleaning from resources and wise counsel, it is you! This is the way you live your life and it has always inspired me. I am so grateful for the many prayers you have prayed for me and over me. I am so grateful that you always followed that up with practicals for me to action. When I was being crushed by life and lost my grip on reality, you made me do homework on vision and perspective; no easy ways out, yet full of grace and understanding. This was a game changer for me! Thank you for agreeing to be a part of this project all the way from Boston! I got a lot of love for ya!

Aunty Mima

I do not think you understand how strategic your part was in making this book a thing. You took me book shopping when I was younger, and you read my scrappy creative pieces. And because of this I knew that you believed in the penman I selectively embraced as I grew up. I remember being bed-bound, wrestling obedience, and you were the one to confirm writing was the right thing to do. Your prayers and lean-in gave me fuel when my tank was empty as the process of writing became less exciting and more excruciating. I am so grateful for you, Aunty. Truly I would not have written this book without you giving gumption to my calling. I love you very much. You are a very special Aunty to me.

Canadian Family – Glendennings, Camerons, Oldfields, Robinsons

Ohhhh Can-a-daaa ... To my Canadian family who embraced me in the thick of my unravelling, I am so grateful for you all! To Mum and Dad, Heather and Gord, thank you for opening your home to me. I came to you very wounded and y'all loved me so well. Thank you for the hugs and the chats by the fireplace. Thank you for the prayers you prayed and continue to pray over me and my family. I flew across the world and found home with you guys.

Kristen! My lovely friend, thank you for cuddles I could collapse in and for not being repelled by my messy life! To Chad and Amanda, Brit and Matt, Chelsea and Dustin, Kara and Courtney, Ashley and Megan, John Cameron, Uncle Manny and quick-wit Mr Robinson. You all gave me incredibly hilarious memories and lots of fun times. Thank you!! Love you guys xx

The crew

To Ambs, Han, Clay, Sly, Jazz, Jarron, Livie, Amelia, Brit and my church fam … THANK YOU! Thank you for the belly laughs, the group chat banter, the copious amounts of Thai food, the laughs, the encouragements, the friendship, the prayers, the support and … the laughs! I am so grateful that during my 'transition' you became my people. I love you guys very much!

ABOUT THE AUTHOR

Brooke Robertson lives in Sydney and describes herself as an introvert with *selective social adaptability*. Having spent six and a half years stroking a competitive ego in the health and fitness industry, she is now trying her hand at telling compelling stories with the intent to provoke thought, share truth and offer hope. Brooke is passionate about building quality friendships, zealously chasing deeper intimacy with God and seeking to live with authenticity. Brooke can be found laughing and eating and most likely dominating a game of Scattergories with her best buds.

9 781922 368485